ArtScroll Mesorah Series®

כוונה

Expositions on Jewish liturgy and thought

Rabbis Nosson Scherman / Meir Zlotowitz
General Editors

tashlich

TASHLICH AND THE THIRTEEN ATTRIBUTES / A
NEW TRANSLATION WITH A COMMENTARY ANTHOLOGIZED
FROM TALMUDIC, MIDRASHIC, AND RABBINIC SOURCES.

Published by

Mesorah Publications, ltd

Translation and Commentary
by
Rabbi Avrohom Chaim Feuer

An Overview / Depths of Repentance
by
Rabbi Nosson Scherman

FIRST EDITION
First Impression . . . August 1979
SECOND EDITION
First Impression . . . July 1980
Second Impression . . . June 1981
Third Impression . . . June 1983
Fourth Impression . . . July 1992
Fifth Impression . . . July 1996
Sixth Impression . . . August 1998

Published and Distributed by
MESORAH PUBLICATIONS, Ltd.
4401 Second Avenue
Brooklyn, New York 11232

Distributed in Europe by
J. LEHMANN HEBREW BOOKSELLERS
20 Cambridge Terrace
Gateshead, Tyne and Wear
England NE8 1RP

Distributed in Israel by
SIFRIATI / A. GITLER – BOOKS
10 Hashomer Street
Bnei Brak 51361

Distributed in Australia & New Zealand by
GOLDS BOOK & GIFT CO.
36 William Street
Balaclava 3183, Vic., Australia

Distributed in South Africa by
KOLLEL BOOKSHOP
Shop 8A Norwood Hypermarket
Norwood 2196, Johannesburg, South Africa

THE ARTSCROLL MESORAH SERIES ®
TASHLICH AND THE THIRTEEN ATTRIBUTES

© Copyright 1979, 1992 by MESORAH PUBLICATIONS, Ltd.
4401 Second Avenue / Brooklyn, N.Y. 11232 / (718) 921-9000

ISBN
0-89906-159-1 (paperback)

Typography by Compuscribe at ArtScroll Studios, Ltd.
4401 Second Avenue / Brooklyn, N.Y. 11232 / (718) 921-9000

Printed in the United States of America by Noble Book Press

✥ An Overview/
   Depths of Repentance

✥ שלש עשרה מדות ✥
   The Thirteen Attributes

An Overview/
Depths of Repentance

I. Abraham's Victory

כְּשֶׁהָלַךְ אַבְרָהָם אָבִינוּ לַעֲקוֹד אֶת יִצְחָק בְּנוֹ הוֹלִיכוֹ הַשָּׂטָן בְּנָהָר עַד שֶׁבָּא עַד צַנָּארוֹ בַּמָּיִם. וְאָמַר אַבְרָהָם: ,,הוֹשִׁיעָה ה׳ כִּי בָאוּ מַיִם עַד נָפֶשׁ!״ וְנִיצוֹל!

When our forefather Abraham went to bind his son, Isaac, [on the altar], Satan led him through a river until the water came up to his neck. Abraham said, 'Help, HASHEM, for water menaces our lives!' Then, he was saved! (Tanchuma, Vayeira 25).

Sons of Prophets

The custom of *Tashlich* is observed wherever there are Jews. Sephardim and Ashkenazim, who had been separated from one another by continents and centuries, all observe *Tashlich*. Yet there is no mention of it in the *Talmud*, or the early *Rishonim*. Even in the *Shulchan Aruch*, it has the barest of mentions (*Rama, Orach Chaim* 583:2). The earliest printed reference to *Tashlich* is in *Maharil*, but he does not say who instituted the practice, only that it is a Jewish custom. *Tashlich* appears to be a manifestation of Israel's genius to devise ways of perfecting itself in the service of God.

Tashlich appears to be a manifestation of Israel's genius to devise ways of perfecting itself in the service of God.

The Sages say: הַנַּח לָהֶם לְיִשְׂרָאֵל, אִם לֹאוּ נְבִיאִים הֵם, בְּנֵי נְבִיאִים הֵם, *Let Israel be, if they are not prophets, they are descendants of prophets* (Pesachim 66a). Indeed, the national soul of Israel has its ways of determining how to draw closer to the service of

God. Commentators have advanced reasons for the custom as we shall see below, but the *primary* reason that *Tashlich* is incumbent upon us is because Israel's usage has ordained the custom's sanctity. As *Rama (Toras HaOlah* 3:56) and *Yosef Ometz* (975) say simply: מִנְהָג יִשְׂרָאֵל תּוֹרָה הוּא, *a custom of Israel has the status of Torah.*

The Satanic River

When Abraham was challenged, Satan had carte blanche *to impede Abraham by weakening his devotion to God.*

Both *Shaloh HaKadosh (Rosh HaShanah, Amod HaDin)* and *Levush (Orach Chaim* 596) cite the same reason for the custom: When Abraham was challenged with the climactic test of his life, God's command to sacrifice Isaac, part of the test was that Satan had *carte blanche* to impede Abraham by weakening his devotion to God. Satan played on the emotions of the aged father who was on the way to give up his beloved heir. Abraham would not be swayed. Finally, Satan placed an impassable river in front of Abraham and Isaac. They forged ahead and went deeper and deeper into the water until it was up to their necks. Abraham was ready to go on — neither logic, water, nor threat of death could deter his resolve, but how could he do God's will if a river were to drown him? He appealed to God, and the river disappeared.

We go to a river to recall before God and to ourselves that our forefather defeated the master of evil at a river.

Abraham's determination had defeated Satan, and he continued unhindered to the summit of devotion to God. The *Tashlich* ritual is intended to recall that climactic episode on the way to the *Akeidah*. We go to a river, or some other body of water, to recall before God and to ourselves, that our forefather defeated the master of evil at a river. Let it remind us of the goal for which we were created, the goal of serving God no matter how potent the force that attempts to dissuade us or force us to do otherwise, no matter how 'impossible' it is to do the right thing, because even the most formidable obstacle is but a test of our devotion. And let it remind God that the spiritual seeds of Abraham are implanted within his children. The merit of the *Akeidah*, therefore, is not a reminder of an ancient, irrelevant event, but an indication of an always present reality of Israel's potential for greatness (see *Overview* to *Vayeira*, ArtScroll *Bereishis* II).

There is a special symbolism in the fact that Satan resorted to a 'river' as his last attempt to force Abraham back. Satan combated Abraham's devotion with the most powerful means at his disposal. According to the *Zohar*, a deep river symbolizes בִּינָה, *understanding*, the ability to plumb the depths of knowledge — to expand, develop and draw conclusions. 'There are waters', the *Zohar* teaches, 'that raise wise people, and there are waters that raise fools.' Understanding is a precious gift of God, but we know all too well how it can be misused and corrupted to give legitimacy and popularity to foolishness and worse. The key to Abraham's greatness was his understanding of truth; destroy that, and he could be pulled down from his spiritual height.

According to the Zohar, a deep river symbolizes בִּינָה, understanding, the ability to plumb the depths of knowledge.

Crisis of Understanding

How does one fight an Abraham? And what was the purpose of the battle? As the *Midrashim* teach, the *Akeidah* was designed to bring into reality an intensified dimension of Abraham's fear of, and devotion to, God. God *knew* what Abraham would do, but human beings are created to act, and, therefore, Abraham had to translate his loyalty into the language of deed in order to reach a higher pinnacle of his greatness. Satan sought to challenge his will, his obedience, his faith. Were Abraham to be prevented from reaching Mount Moriah by wild horses, tidal waves, and stone walls, Satan would not have made his point. He would have made it physically impossible for a human being to fulfill God's will, but he would not have proven the person's unwillingness to sacrifice everything for the sake of God.

Abraham had to translate his loyalty into the language of deed in order to reach a higher pinnacle of his greatness.

In this perspective, we must understand the Satanic river impeding Abraham's progress. Ultimately, the river symbolized the deepest level of understanding, the inexorable intelligence that cried out against every step that Abraham took, saying: 'Isaac is your only heir! You waited a lifetime for

Ultimately, the river symbolized the deepest level of understanding, the inexorable intelligence that cried out against every step that Abraham took.

him! God delivered him to you and Sarah by means of miracles. God promised you posterity through him. How can you, who preached against human sacrifice, slaughter your own son? How can an old father kill his only son with his own hands? How can you obey — *even believe in* — the God Who demands this of you?'

These questions constitute a 'river' more torrential than any on earth. We can more easily picture Abraham walking across the Amazon at its deepest than we can perceive him negotiating this river of understanding that defied his every attempt to comprehend God's purpose.

Abraham responded with an even higher level of understanding than Satan's. He called out to God for help,

'The waters of understanding are up to my neck. They threaten to drown my limited human intelligence. Nevertheless, I know that רֵאשִׁית חָכְמָה יִרְאַת ה', *the beginning of wisdom is fear of HASHEM* (*Psalms* 112:10); the source of wisdom is not what my mortal mind conceives, nor the overwhelmingly compelling logic of Satan. I cannot refute his arguments nor cross his river, because my humanity limits me. But *You*, HASHEM, — *You* are my Guide, and when all else fails me, I negate my wisdom to Your will.'

By plunging into the river that produced fools, Abraham transformed the event into a river that produced within him — and his offspring — a heightened perception of Israel's mission.

The river disappeared. By plunging into the river that produced fools, Abraham transformed the event into a river that produced within him — and his offspring — a heightened perception of Israel's mission, for to experience truth is far more fulfilling than to philosophize about it.

To remember this lesson, *Shaloh* and *Levush* teach, the Jewish nation repairs to its rivers and waterways during the most solemn and awesome period of the year. Exactly when and where the first Jews went to the first *Tashlich* we do not know, but it was almost certainly during the Middle Ages when pogrom, inquisition, death, torture and expulsion were the daily lot of the Jew. One can easily imagine Satan throwing a river of tears and blood in the path of our ancestors and asking questions hardly less difficult than those he asked Abraham. Jews

There is an understanding more compelling than Satan's, an understanding that transcends the narrow limits of human intelligence.

responded as they always have. There is an understanding more compelling than Satan's, an understanding that transcends the narrow limits of human intelligence. 'Help us, HASHEM, as You helped Abraham, from the waters that threaten to inundate our faith, because, like our father, we place our faith in You above all else.'

The Coronation

It is a throwback to the ancient custom of Scriptural times when it was customary to crown new kings at river banks.

In this perspective, we can better understand another reason given for the *Tashlich* custom. *Siddur Otzar HaTefillos* submits that it is a throwback to the ancient custom of Scriptural times when it was customary to crown new kings at river banks. Rosh HaShanah is the day when God stands revealed as the *King* Who judges His universe and holds its destiny in His hand. Our prayers begin to incorporate this concept on Rosh HaShanah when we describe Him as הַמֶּלֶךְ הַקָּדוֹשׁ, *the Holy King*. The *Musaf Shemoneh Esrei* includes ten Scriptural verses attesting to His Kingship. *R' Saadiah Gaon* comments that one reason for the *shofar* blast is to approximate the trumpeting tribute to a monarch.

We trek to a river to crown God, as it were.

Therefore, declares *Otzar HaTefillos*, we trek to a river to crown God, as it were, in the ancient manner of servants accepting upon themselves the sovereignty of their ruler. The *Ten Sefiros* [Emanations] conclude with מַלְכוּת, *Kingship*, the manifestation on earth of God's total mastery of creation. Abraham's tenth trial, the *Akeidah*, was simultaneously the culminating demonstration of his greatness and of God's revelation in human events (see *Overviews* to *Lech Lecha* and *Vayeira*, *Bereishis II*; and to *Ruth*). Abraham's conquest of the river of misunderstanding was a key element of this manifestation of God's majesty; therefore, it is commemorated by *Tashlich* on the very day God is acknowledged as King.

Abraham's conquest of the river of misunderstanding was a key element of this manifestation of God's majesty.

II. The Eternal Akeidah*

ר' חֲנִינָה בֶּן דּוֹסָא אוֹמֵר: אוֹתוֹ הָאַיִל לֹא יָצָא
מִמֶּנּוּ דָבָר לְבַטָלָה. אֶפְרוֹ שֶׁל אַיִל הוּא יְסוֹד שֶׁעַל
גַּבֵּי מִזְבֵּחַ הַפְּנִימִי ... גִּידָיו שֶׁל אַיִל הֵם עֲשָׂרָה
כְּנֶגֶד עֲשָׂרָה נִימִין שֶׁל כִּנּוֹר שֶׁהָיָה דָוִד מְנַגֵּן
בָּהֶם...עוֹרוֹ שֶׁל אַיִל הוּא אֵזוֹר מָתְנָיו שֶׁל אֵלִיָהוּ
... שְׁתֵּי קַרְנָיו שֶׁל אַיִל, שֶׁל שְׂמֹאל נִשְׁמַע קוֹלוֹ
עַל הַר סִינַי וְקֶרֶן שֶׁל יָמִין הוּא גָדוֹל מִן הַשְּׂמֹאל,
וְעָתִיד לִתְקוֹעַ בּוֹ לְעָתִיד לָבֹא בְּקִבּוּץ שֶׁל גָּלֻיוֹת.
R'Chaninah ben Dosa says: No part of
that ram [which Abraham used as a
sacrifice at the Akeidah in place of Isaac]
went unused. The ashes of the ram were in
the top of the inner altar ... the veins of the
ram were ten, corresponding to the ten
strings of the harp upon which David
played... The skin of the ram was the
leather belt girdling Elijah's loins ... As for
the two horns of the ram, the sound of the
left one was heard [as the shofar sound] on
Mount Sinai, and the right horn is greater
than the left one, and it will be blown in
the time to Come when all exiles are
gathered together (Pirkei d'Rabbi Eliezer
ch. 31).

A Compensatory Deed

Let us attempt to conceive of all the Jewish spiritual accomplishments of the nearly thirty-seven centuries since the Akeidah.

Abraham's primary test at the *Akeidah* was the realization that he was to forfeit God's promise that Israel would descend from him. Were the childless Isaac to die, Abraham's life-dream would forever go unrealized. Let us attempt to conceive of all the Jewish spiritual accomplishments of the nearly thirty-seven centuries since the *Akeidah*. Surely an impossible task! All the Torah, all the *mitzvos*, all the holiness, all the kindness! Thirty-seven centuries worth of achievement by all the hundreds of millions of Jews who have lived since the *Akeidah!* Abraham

* [This section of the *Overview* is based on a *shiur* given by Harav Gedaliah Schorr זצ"ל.]

Abraham was ready to substitute one stroke of the knife for all that.

was ready to substitute one stroke of the knife for all that, if such were God's wish.

Let us view Abraham's potential deed from another perspective. We know that in the world of the spirit, the *quality* of a single *mitzvah* can often outweigh many, many others. As Abraham advanced upon Mount Moriah, he recognized that the one deed he was preparing to perform would have to be of sufficient quality and of such significance that it would be equivalent of all the centuries of Jewish life that would never be. There could be no other *spiritual* explanation of the slaughter of the one person who was intended to be the forerunner of God's Chosen people.

The realization was alluded to in Abraham's statement to his servants as he took leave of them and went with Isaac to the summit of Mount Moriah: אֲנִי וְהַנַּעַר נֵלְכָה עַד כֹּה, *I and the youth* [i.e., *Isaac*] *will go* [כֹּה] *yonder* [lit. *thus*]. *Rashi* comments that the word כֹּה alludes to the earlier promise God had given Abraham: כֹּה יִהְיֶה זַרְעֶךָ, *thus* [like the infinite number of the stars] *will your children be (Gen. 15:6).* As Abraham went up the mountain to offer Isaac as a sacrifice, he had in mind the infinite accomplishments expected of his posterity. He perceived that his one act would have to be the spiritual equivalent of the billions upon billions of good deeds that would never be done. The purpose of Israel's existence is to manifest the majesty of God as King — Abraham, by his conquest of Satan and of his own human, intelligent and paternal feelings, would demonstrate that the only determining factor is the will of the King.

He perceived that his one act would have to be the spiritual equivalent of the billions upon billions of good deeds that would never be done.

As the event developed, however, the *Akeidah* was not to replace Jewish history. Instead, it was to be a seminal event in the very creation of that history because his devotion then, created the pattern of self-sacrifice and courage that has characterized Jewry ever since. Not only has it affected Jewish behavior, but it remains a source of merit for every Jew who has within his heart an ember of the *Akeidah* (*Sfas Emes*).

A Seminal Event

By investing his act with the intention of compensating for an immense future history that might never be, he added new dimensions to those events of the future.

With this perspective we can better comprehend the disposition of every part of Abraham's ram. His deed did not end when he and Isaac descended the mountain leaving the smoldering ashes of the ram behind him on the altar. By investing his act with the intention of compensating for an immense future history that might never be, he added new dimensions to — perhaps even made possible — those events of the future. This, then, is the deeper meaning of *Pirkei D'Rabbi Eliezer* cited above:

— The corners of the Inner Altar upon which the *Kohen Gadol* would sprinkle blood of atonement on Yom Kippur, contained the spiritual presence of the ultimate sacrifice Abraham was prepared to make — and, therefore, Israel remains more deserving of atonement even when it falls short of the standard it is meant to achieve.

— David's harp, which played the Sweet Singer's eternal songs of devotion, was strung with the devotion represented by Abraham's ram. Great though he was, without an Abraham there could not have been a David of such stature.

— Elijah girded himself with bravery to defy King Ahab and Queen Jezebel, and their false prophets. By his example he was able to induce all Israel to declare ה׳ הוּא אֱלֹהִים, ה׳ הוּא אֱלֹהִים, *HASHEM — He is God! HASHEM — He is God (I Kings 18:39)!* Elijah succeeded in eliciting this recognition from Israel because he clothed himself with Abraham's manifestation of God's Kingship.

Elijah succeeded in eliciting this recognition from Israel because he clothed himself with Abraham's manifestation of God's Kingship.

— God's Presence on Sinai was proclaimed by a powerful, incessant *shofar* blast. Hearing its call, Israel accepted, and dedicated itself to, the Torah. That resolve, too, was a legacy of Abraham. The *shofar* sound of Sinai alluded to the left and lesser horn of Abraham's ram. The day at Sinai was the lesser of the two greatest days in history, because Israel was not yet fully ready to play the role assigned it. But that day will come ...

The shofar of Moshiach will be the right horn of Abraham's ram that will summon even the forlorn and assimilated exiles from earth's most forsaken lands.

— The *shofar* of *Moshiach* will be the right horn of Abraham's ram. That will be the שׁוֹפָר גָּדוֹל, *great shofar*, that will summon even the forlorn and as-

similated exiles from earth's most forsaken lands.
Then they will come to Jerusalem, to the mountain of
God, to Mount Moriah where Abraham stood at the
Akeidah and sanctified the present and future for all
time.

This is a further manifestation of the principle of
מַעֲשֵׂי אָבוֹת סִימָן לַבָּנִים , *the deeds of the Patriarchs are
portents for the children* (see *Overview* to *Lech
Lecha*, ArtScroll *Bereishis* II). The lives of their
posterity indeed reflect the experiences of the
Patriarchs, but to view this phenomenon as an in-
stance of history repeating itself is so superficial as to
miss the point entirely. When a seed develops into a
plant, history has not merely repeated itself; the seed
has *produced* the plant. A bushel of kernels produces
a field of grain. Abraham's deeds were the seeds that
grew into service at an altar, songs on a harp, courage
on a mountain, the announcement of mankind's
destiny, the call of creation's fulfillment.

When Jews stand in repentance at a river bank, they are Abraham advancing to an angry river and erasing every question mark seeking to cloud his faith.

When Jews stand in repentance at a river bank, an
ocean beach, a backyard well, and repent with their
Tashlich prayer, they are Abraham advancing into
an angry river and erasing every question mark seeking to cloud his faith.

III. Lesson of the Depths

T he core of the *Tashlich* prayer is the selection of
three verses from *Micah* (7:18-20) which ask the
Merciful God to cast Israel's sins בִּמְצֻלוֹת יַם, *into the
depths of the sea* (see *comm.* to *Tashlich*). *Rama* in
Toras HaOlah finds in this expression a primary
reason for the *Tashlich* custom.

The seas are by far the greater part of earth. The
waters should have inundated the land and made
human life impossible. Indeed, storms and tidal
waves give us continuous reminders of the ocean's
awesome power. At the beginning of creation, water
covered everything; there was no dry land at all until

God commanded that the waters congregate to form seas and expose the land.

That God created an overwhelming mass of water but decreed the emergence of lands, reveals that the purpose of creation was to provide a habitat for man, a setting where he could exercise his Divinely given intelligence and let his soul be master of his body in God's service. Rosh HaShanah inaugurates the days when man is judged by his Maker. How well has he served God? How well has he utilized the earth and its fullness that God placed at his disposal? How well has he achieved the purpose of his existence?

The purpose of creation was to provide a habitat for man, a setting where he could exercise his Divinely given intelligence.

Standing before the watery deep on the Day of Judgment, a Jew is reawakened to his mission on earth. The commentators cite the further symbolism of having fish in the water at which *Tashlich* is recited (see *Shaloh; Magen Avraham 583; Ketzei HaMateh* to *Mateh Ephraim 598*). The defenseless fish, prey to every net and hook, remind man that he, too, has no guarantee of safety. The unblinking eyes of the fish suggest the eternally vigilant and merciful eye of God. The fish, covered by the waters and safe from the evil eye of jealousy allude to Israel which has been granted God's blessing of protection.

So many reminders. So many prods to the conscience, sensitivity, and awareness of the Jew.

So many reminders. So many prods to the conscience, sensitivity, and awareness of the Jew. So much that unites him as a branch with the Abrahamitic seed from which he sprang. How sad that people, as creatures of habit, are so apt to clutch at ritual and neglect its purpose.

His ancestor once confronted a Satanic river, but refused to let his resolve buckle; and by doing so, he planted a seed whose fruits we still harvest.

But no matter what has occurred over so many years and in so many lands, the Jew is reminded on Rosh HaShanah, or on whatever other day he goes to *Tashlich*, that his ancestor once confronted a Satanic river, but refused to let his resolve buckle; and by doing so, he planted a seed whose fruits we still harvest.

Rabbi Nosson Scherman

י״ג מִדּוֹת / The Thirteen Attributes of Mercy

At Sinai, Israel pledged eternal devotion to the Creator of heaven and earth, but forty days later, Israel betrayed this promise and offered allegiance to the Golden Calf.

The Almighty wished to annihilate the treacherous nation in a single moment of terrible retribution. Only the impassioned protests of Moses turned God's anger to mercy.

The climax of the pardon came in a new revelation to Moses as God passed before him, and Moses was shown שְׁלֹשׁ עֶשְׂרֵה מִדּוֹת שֶׁל רַחֲמִים, *the Thirteen Attributes of Mercy:*

ה׳ ה׳ אֵל רַחוּם וְחַנּוּן אֶרֶךְ אַפַּיִם וְרַב חֶסֶד וֶאֱמֶת. נֹצֵר חֶסֶד לָאֲלָפִים נֹשֵׂא עָוֹן וָפֶשַׁע וְחַטָּאָה וְנַקֵּה לֹא יְנַקֶּה פֹּקֵד עֲוֹן אָבוֹת עַל בָּנִים וְעַל בְּנֵי בָנִים עַל שִׁלֵּשִׁים וְעַל רִבֵּעִים.

HASHEM, HASHEM, God, Merciful and Compassionate, Slow to Anger, and Abundant in Kindness and Truth. Preserver of Kindness for thousands of generations, Forgiver of Iniquity, Transgression and Sin. He Who Erases and He does not erase. He accounts the iniquities of fathers to their children and their children's children to the third and fourth generation (Exodus 34:6-7).

✥ The Guarantee

אָמַר רַבִּי יוֹחָנָן: מְלַמֵּד שֶׁנִּתְעַטֵּף הַקָּבָּ״ה כִּשְׁלִיחַ צִבּוּר, וְהֶרְאָה לוֹ לְמֹשֶׁה סֵדֶר תְּפִלָּה. אָמַר לוֹ: כָּל זְמַן שֶׁיִּשְׂרָאֵל חוֹטְאִין, יַעֲשׂוּ לְפָנַי כְּסֵדֶר הַזֶּה, וַאֲנִי מוֹחֵל לָהֶם... אָמַר רַבִּי יְהוּדָה: בְּרִית כְּרוּתָה לִשְׁלֹשׁ עֶשְׂרֵה מִדּוֹת שֶׁאֵינָם חוֹזְרוֹת רֵיקָם, שֶׁנֶּאֱמַר: (שמות לד:י) הִנֵּה אָנֹכִי כֹּרֵת בְּרִית.

R' Yochanan said: Scripture teaches that the Holy One, Blessed be He, wrapped Himself in a prayer shawl like a chazan and showed Moses the order of prayer. God said to him, 'Whenever Israel sins, let them perform this order of service and I will forgive them...'

R' Yehudah said: A covenant has been struck that the Thirteen Attributes are never turned back unanswered, as Scripture states (Exodus 34:10): Behold I [God] strike a covenant [Rosh HaShanah 17b].

What is the nature of this covenant?

The *Brisker Rav* explains that it was as if God assembled an enormous cache of mercy. From this treasure-house of kindness, He would forever withdraw whatever was needed in response to Israel's invocation of the Thirteen Attributes (*Chiddushei Griz HaLevi, Ki Sisa*). For this reason, any plea for the mercy guaranteed in the Thirteen Attributes *must* be answered — because there is always an ample supply of mercy available for those in need.

Mercy Under Control

There are many laws in the Torah designed to prevent cruelty to living things. The *mishnah* (*Berachos* 5:3) cautions, however: Do not say, 'God's mercy is so great that He pities even little birds,' because such a statement wrongly ascribes merciful traits to God, while God's attributes are actually strict decrees (*Berachos* 33b).

Yad HaMelech (*Rambam, Hilchos Tefillah* 9:7) explains that God's mercy is totally different from the mercy of man. Man is swayed by his emotions. He takes pity on the plight of those who suffer because he cannot stand the sight of pain.

In contrast, God's mercy emanates from His *power* rather than from weakness. God is in complete control of His reactions to the sufferings of all forms of life. The very concept of emotion does not apply to God, for it is His supreme intellect which motivates His decision to show mercy. Sometimes, God's infinite wisdom decrees that the cure for an individual's suffering is the harshness of דִּין, *justice*, rather than mercy. In all cases, God's supreme intelligence decrees what will come to pass; it is only in our perception that His acts are seen to be good or bad.

Therefore, concludes *Yad HaMelech*, the exalted attribute of mercy is called אֵל, literally, *Powerful One* [see *Rashi, Exodus* 15:11], to denote that God's mercy derives from His intellectual strength, rather than from emotional weakness.

Indeed, the *Brisker Rav* (*Chiddushei HaGriz HaLevi, Parshas Noach*) cites *Rambam's* teaching (*Hilchos Yesodei HaTorah* 1:1) that God is far removed from emotions such as mercy, which pertain only to corporeal bodies. The correct perception of Divine mercy is described in the Rosh HaShanah liturgy where God is described as פּוֹעֵל רַחֲמָיו בַּדִּין, *He who 'activates' His mercy at the Time of Judgment*. This means that there is a heavenly force of mercy, not of God's essence but controlled by Him, and which He *activates* when He deems it proper to do so.

Imitate His Ways

אָמַר לוֹ: כָּל זְמַן שֶׁיִּשְׂרָאֵל חוֹטְאִין, יַעֲשׂוּ לְפָנַי כְּסֵדֶר הַזֶּה, וַאֲנִי מוֹחֵל לָהֶם
God said to Moses, 'Whenever Israel sins, let them perform this order of service before Me and I will forgive them' (Rosh HaShanah 17a).

Is the recitation of the Thirteen Attributes a magic formula which miraculously erases sin without any further effort? Is God so easily appeased?

In fact, God was very precise and explicit in establishing the conditions of this covenant. He did not say יֹאמְרוּ לְפָנַי, *let them 'recite' before Me*. Rather, He said, יַעֲשׂוּ לְפָנַי, *let them 'perform' before Me*, this order of service. In order to activate God's mercy, Jews must *act* in accordance with God's Attributes; in their relationship with their fellow man, they must conduct themselves with a degree of mercy worthy of Him.

The Torah commands: וְהָלַכְתָּ בִּדְרָכָיו, *And you shall follow in His ways* (*Deuteronomy* 28:9). The Rabbis expound: Just as He is called Compassionate, so should you be compassionate. Just as He is called Merciful, so should you be merciful. Just as He is called Holy, so should you be holy. In this fashion, the prophets referred to God with many designations such as Slow to Anger, Abundant in Mercy, Righteous, Upright, Perfect, Powerful, and Strong. They used these descriptions to indicate that these are the proper examples to follow. Therefore, a person must emulate God as much as he possibly can... He who follows this path brings goodness and blessing upon himself (*Rambam, Hilchos Deos* 1:6,7).

Indeed, *Shaloh HaKadosh* (*Shaar HaOsios*) perceives man's fulfillment of the Thirteen Attributes as a cardinal act of faith. *Shaloh* demonstrates that God's Thirteen Attributes correspond to the Thirteen Articles of Faith in God as delineated by *Rambam*. The man who merges his entire being with the Divine model of mercy simultaneously achieves an unprecedented level of pure faith.

←§ Significance of Thirteen

The number thirteen is very significant. The numerical value of אֶחָד, one, equals thirteen [ד=4; ח=8; א=1], and teaches us that whoever concentrates the faith of his heart on the One and Only God, deserves to be treated according to the Thirteen Attributes of Divine Mercy. The Hebrew names of the Patriarchs — אַבְרָהָם, יִצְחָק, יַעֲקֹב — contain a total of thirteen letters, and the tribes of Israel (including Menashe and Ephraim) are thirteen, to teach that whoever recites these Thirteen Attributes with complete devotion will gain the merit of the virtuous Patriarchs and the thirteen tribes [Sefer Milchemes Mitzvah; Intro. to Sefer HaMeoros on Berachos by R' Meir ben Moshe HaMeili].

All commentators agree that the number of Divine Attributes is thirteen, but there are a variety of opinions as to the precise identification of these attributes. Most commentators follow the view of Rabbeinu Tam (Tosafos, Rosh HaShanah 17b). His approach will be followed here.

ה' ה' — HASHEM, HASHEM.

God's willingness to forgive and to accept the penitent is the function of His Four-Letter Name — the Name that designates His merciful attribute. This Name [from the letters of הָיָה הֹוֶה וְיִהְיֶה, He was, is, and will be] designates God as the מְהַוֶּה, Prime Cause, of all that is present in creation. Since the Creator is the Father of all that exists, it is only natural that He wishes to assure the survival of all that He brought into being (Milchemes Mitzvah).

The Four-Letter Name expresses God's timelessness. Though man may sin, he can repent and call upon the timeless God to restore him to his original innocent state. As the Talmud states: ה' ה': אֲנִי הוּא קוֹדֶם שֶׁיֶּחֱטָא הָאָדָם, וַאֲנִי הוּא לְאַחַר שֶׁיֶּחֱטָא הָאָדָם, וְיַעֲשֶׂה תְּשׁוּבָה, HASHEM, HASHEM (Exodus 34:6): I am He [i.e., the God of Mercy] before a person sins, and I am He after a person sins and repents (Rosh HaShanah 17b).

Based on this dictum, Rabbeinu Tam counts ה' ה' as two separate attributes: 1) the mercy God displays before someone sins; and 2) the mercy He displays after he sins.

This statement is a source of puzzlement for many commentators. Why does a person require mercy even before he sins?

Rosh explains that although the Omniscient God sees the future clearly and knows that one has within him the evil that will develop into a sinful deed, God ignores this foreknowledge and treats him according to his present condition of innocence.

Harav Gifter cites the Talmudic dictum (Kiddushin 30b) that the Evil Inclination renews its vigor daily and threatens to overwhelm man. Without Divine assistance, no man could withstand its assault. Thus, HASHEM dispenses mercy before the sin by providing man the moral fortitude which enables him to resist temptation.

R' Saadiah Gaon (cited by Ibn Ezra, Exodus 34:6) and R' Nissim Gaon (quoted by Tosafos and Rosh, Rosh HaShanah 17b) differ from Rabbeinu Tam. They maintain that the first mention of ה' is not a description of HASHEM at all. In their interpretation God Himself, not Moses, announced the Thirteen Attributes. The first ה', they contend, should be read together with the words which precede it: וַיַּעֲבֹר ה' עַל פָּנָיו וַיִּקְרָא ה', And HASHEM passed before him [Moses], and HASHEM called out.

ARIzal begins the Thirteen Attributes with אֵל and does not reckon either mention of the Four-Letter Name in the total of thirteen.

Sefer Chassidim (250) begins his calculation from רַחוּם and deletes the three Names ה' ה' אֵל, from the count [see Korban Nesanel, Rosh, Rosh HaShanah 7b]. This concurs with the opinion of Meiri [Chibbur HaTeshuvah 2:9].

אֵל — God.

This is the third Attribute according to Rabbeinu Tam. This Name, too, denotes Divine mercy, but on a level of intensity which far surpasses the mercy designated by the Name *HASHEM* (*Rashi*).

This powerful degree of mercy is reserved exclusively for the very righteous who err without intending to flout God's will, and repent immediately. These pure souls are still considered the sons of the מְהַוֶּה, *Prime Cause*. Therefore, God will exert Himself, as it were, to assure their survival. God's mercy for them is so powerful that He even disregards the laws of nature for their sake and performs miracles of salvation (*Melchemes Mitzvah*).

רַחוּם — *Merciful.*

This is the fourth attribute. It is exercised on behalf of those who are found guilty in God's judgment. They will be punished, but if they call out to God for mercy, He will ease the intensity of their suffering (*Sforno, Exodus 34:6*).

Alternatively, this attribute refers to God's mercy in averting moments of crisis or temptation that overpower one's normal degree of self-control. Thus, this attribute is of a relatively mild intensity, for it is the mercy that God shows *before* a person is criticially engulfed in a situation beyond his control (gloss to *Tosafos, Rosh HaShanah* 17b).

וְחַנּוּן — *And Compassionate.*

This is the fifth attribute. The root of חַנּוּן is חֵן, *charm*, which is related to חִנָּם, *free of charge.* God is compassionate and aids even those unworthy of His kindness. If they make a sincere request, God responds although they lack the merit with which to 'pay' for His kindness (see *Berachos* 7a).

Unlike the fourth attribute רַחוּם, *Merciful*, which is exercised *before* a crisis, the attribute חַנּוּן is exercised *during* a crisis. The compassionate God does not ignore the cries and pleas of the person seeking to avoid sin when his own will-power is unequal to the task. God rescues him, although he is unworthy of such aid (gloss to *Tosafos, Rosh HaShanah* 17b).

The *Midrash* (*Shemos Rabbah* 45:6) relates that God revealed to Moses the treasury of Divine gifts, as it were. Moses asked God to identify each type of gift. God responded, 'This treasure is for those who faithfully observe My *mitzvos*. This treasure is for those who raise orphans.' So it continued from chest to chest, until Moses saw a huge chest. God explained, 'This treasure chest is reserved for those who are undeserving. If I desire to assist them חִנָּם, *free of charge*, [i.e., though they are undeserving], I take a portion from here.' *Etz Yosef* explains that this chest is huge because most people do not merit Divine help.

אֶרֶךְ אַפַּיִם — *Slow to Anger.*

This is the sixth attribute. Literally, אֶרֶךְ means *long*, to signify that God is not short-tempered. He takes a *long* time to grow angry, in order to afford the sinner an opportunity to repent before it is too late (*Rashi*).

Rabbeinu Tam counts אֶרֶךְ אַפַּיִם as one attribute. However, the gloss to *Tosafos* and *Rabbeinu Bachya* (*Kad HaKemach, Os Kippurim*) consider this as two attributes, because God is patient with the righteous in one way and shows forebearance to the wicked in a different manner.

Tosafos (*Eruvin* 22a) explains that אַפַּיִם is the plural of אַף, *countenance, face*. [Literally, אַף means *nose* which is the most prominent feature of the face.] God has two 'faces': to the wicked man He displays a benign, smiling face and showers him with prosperity. He displays this אַף for a long time until the wicked man dies without repentance and suffers eternal damnation.

To the righteous man, however, God displays an angry countenance. He grows wrathful and punishes his slight sins in This World. He waits אֶרֶךְ, *a long time*, before rewarding him for his good deeds. Finally, however, after having purged the righteous person of sin in This World, God smilingly gives him his eternal reward in the World to Come.

וְרַב חֶסֶד — *And Abundant in Kindness.*

This is the seventh attribute. It is directed toward those who lack personal merits. God compensates for their deficiency with His abundant store of kindness (*Rashi*).

If the scales of justice are exactly balanced and a man's merits and sins are equal, God, in His abundant kindness, will tilt the scales in favor of the side of merit (Rosh HaShanah 17a).

Some say that God's kindness consists of disregarding the first two sins a person commits [מַעֲבִיר רִאשׁוֹן רִאשׁוֹן, He overlooks the first two (lit., the first, the first)]. Later, at the time of the annual accounting on Rosh HaShanah, God places all subsequent sins on the scales. If all the merits outweigh the subsequent demerits, then God discards the first two sins forever. But, if the subsequent demerits equal the merits, then this person is deemed unworthy of God's abundant kindness. God then recalls the first two sins, places them on the scale, and the demerits outweigh the merits (Rif, Rosh HaShanah 17a).

וֶאֱמֶת — And Truth.

This is the eighth attribute. It signifies that God insures that His promises are fulfilled. He never reneges on His word and can be trusted to reward the deserving (Rashi).

נֹצֵר חֶסֶד לָאֲלָפִים — Preserver of Kindness for thousands of generations.

This is the ninth attribute. The descendants of the righteous man will benefit from the merit of their ancestor for two thousand generations, on the condition that they follow his righteous example.

In Deuteronomy 7:9, however, Scripture says that merit extends only for one thousand generations. The Talmud (Sotah 31a) explains that the merit of those who serve God out of intense love lasts two thousand generations, but the merit of those who serve Him out of fear lasts only for one thousand.

According to the commentators who count 'ה 'ה as only one attribute, this attribute is reckoned as two. First, God is נֹצֵר חֶסֶד, Preserver of Kindness, from one generation to the next, from father to son. Secondly, He does this up to two thousand generations, whereas the remembrance of iniquity continues only for רְבֵעִים, four generations, if children emulate the evil of their fathers. This teaches that God's reward exceeds His punishment by a ratio of five hundred to one; i.e., although He limits punishment to four generations, He extends

kindness to two thousand.

נֹשֵׂא עָוֹן — Forgiver of Iniquity.

This is the tenth attribute. An עָוֹן is a sin committed intentionally because of lust or desire. If the offender repents, God will forgive him.

וָפֶשַׁע — (Forgiver of) Transgression.

This is the eleventh attribute. A פֶשַׁע is a sin committed with the intention of defying and angering God. If the transgressor is sincere in his regret and in his resolve never to repeat the sin in the future, God will forgive even so serious an offense.

וְחַטָּאָה — And (Forgiver of) Sin.

This is the twelfth attribute. A חֵטְא is a sin committed carelessly, but unintentionally. God forgives the sinner who repents.

A question can be raised: If we already know that God forgives even intentional sins, does it not go without saying that He also forgives unintentional sins?

The order of these offenses in the Thirteen Attributes alludes to Moses' plea: 'O Lord, when Israel is guilty of iniquity and rebellion, accept their penitence and consider their serious transgressions as merely accidental sins' (Yoma 36b). Thus Moses asked that God overlook the severity of their brazen sins and treat them as if they were committed unintentionally. Thereafter, a plea is made that forgiveness be granted for unintentional sins.

Abarbanel considers נֹשֵׂא עָוֹן וָפֶשַׁע וְחַטָּאָה as one attribute, not three.

וְנַקֵּה לֹא יְנַקֶּה — He Who Erases and He does not erase.

This is the thirteenth attribute. God wipes away the sins of those who repent, but does not wipe away the sins of those who refuse to repent (Yoma 86a).

Alternatively, when God erases sins, He does so gradually, [i.e., He erases, but He does not erase completely] in order to save the sinner from being overwhelmed by the sudden and enormous degree of suffering that may be necessary to atone for the full measure of his sin. Therefore, He erases the sin bit by bit so that whatever punishment

He deems necessary will be bearable (Rashi).

Rabbeinu Bachya says that this refers to sins committed secretly (Bava Kamma 79b). [Such sins are very severe because they indicate that although the sinner is afraid to sin in the presence of man, he has no fear of the Omnipresent God.]

Psalms 19:14 contains the plea, מִנִּסְתָּרוֹת נַקֵּנִי, from hidden sins cleanse me. This thirteenth attribute assures that God will erase and clean away even hidden sin.

R' Alfas (Rosh HaShanah 17a) cites R' Hai Gaon, who reckons וְנַקֵּה לֹא יְנַקֶּה as two separate attributes. This is also the opinion of Abarbanel, who reckons ה' ה' as a single attribute, and נֹשֵׂא עָוֹן וָפֶשַׁע וְחַטָּאָה as only one attribute. In addition, Abarbanel counts פּוֹקֵד עֲוֹן אָבוֹת as an attribute.

Sefer Chassidim counts וְסָלַחְתָּ לַעֲוֹנֵנוּ וּלְחַטָּאתֵנוּ וּנְחַלְתָּנוּ, You pardon our iniquities and our sins and make us Your heritage (Exodus 34:9) as three attributes.

◈§ The Abridged Order

After the Golden Calf, Israel's second great sin was the acceptance of the evil report of the מְרַגְלִים, spies, who spoke disparagingly of the Holy Land. Again, God wished to destroy the Jews, but Moses invoked Divine Mercy and cried out:

ה' אֶרֶךְ אַפַּיִם וְרַב חֶסֶד נֹשֵׂא עָוֹן וָפֶשַׁע וְנַקֵּה לֹא יְנַקֶּה פֹּקֵד עֲוֹן אָבוֹת עַל בָּנִים עַל
שִׁלֵּשִׁים וְעַל רִבֵּעִים.

HASHEM, Slow to Anger, Abundant in Kindness, Bearer of Iniquity and Transgression, He Erases and He does not erase, he accounts the iniquity of the fathers to the sons, to the third generation and the fourth generation (Numbers 14:18).

Many of the original Thirteen Attributes were omitted from Moses' prayer. Ramban (Numbers 14:18) explains that after this second sin, God was far angrier than He was after the first sin. Since Moses knew that God was not inclined to exercise full mercy, he did not invoke all of God's merciful qualities. Primarily, Moses pleaded with God to be אֶרֶךְ אַפַּיִם, slow to anger, so that He would not destroy them instantly but would allow the guilty to perish gradually throughout the forty years in the wilderness. Moses omitted one mention of ה', HASHEM, אֵל, God, רחום, Merciful, חַנּוּן, Compassionate, because God had manifested Himself as the Dispenser of Strict Justice rather than as the Dispenser of Mercy. [Moses did not invoke אֱמֶת, truth, because according to the strict dictates of truth, the Jews deserved to die.] No reference is made to Preservers of Kindness for thousands of generations, for that is a reference to the merit of the Patriarchs, which Israel had forfeited by its lack of faith. The Patriarchs dedicated themselves to acquiring the Holy Land as an estate for their descendants, yet these descendants had rejected and despised the Holy Land — an act tantamount to rejecting the merits of their forefathers.

Finally, Moses did not ask God to be נֹשֵׂא...חַטָּאָה, Forgiver of unintentional sin, because Israel had defied God intentionally and rebelliously.

◈§ The Supreme Attributes

The Zohar (Parshas Naso 131) reveals that there are two series of Divine attributes. Those which were promulgated through Moses are called לְתַתָּא, lower ones. A higher level of mercy was pronounced in the prophecy of Micah, who introduced תְּלֵיסַר מְכִילִין דְרַחֲמֵי עִילָאִין, Thirteen Tiaras of 'Supreme' Mercy. These two levels of Divine mercy are found respectively in the prophetic expressions of Moses and Micah, each of whom spoke of Thirteen Attributes of Mercy.

Moses spoke when Israel was being judged severely for the great sin of the Golden Calf. Therefore, Moses cast God in the role of the strict judge who can mellow his verdict and temper harshness with compassion. Micah, however, spoke of God's mercy in its purest form; the mercy He practices when He is pleased with Israel.

At the conclusion of his prophecy, Micah foretells the glorious future of Israel: כִּימֵי צֵאתְךָ מֵאֶרֶץ מִצְרָיִם אַרְאֶנּוּ נִפְלָאוֹת, *As in the days when you went forth from Egypt, I shall show them wonders (Micah 7:15).*

The sins of Israel initiated their exile. When these sins are forgiven, Israel will return *(Ibn Ezra; Radak).* Then God will activate a measure of compassion which will surpass even the compassion described in Moses' Thirteen Attributes of Mercy *(Malbim).*

The Thirteen *Supreme* Attributes enumerated by Micah parallel the original, lower ones and loosely correspond to them. However, the precise relationship of the two series is discussed only in the mystical literature of *Kabbalah,* and is beyond the scope of this work.

In traditional *Machzorim* [High Holy Days prayerbooks], each of the Thirteen Attributes of Moses is printed in small type above the corresponding attribute in the Thirteen of Micah. This formula follows *ARIzal's* accounting of the Attributes.

These verses from *Micah* form the very core of the *Tashlich* service.

An interpretation of the second series of attributes is the theme of the classical work *Tomer Devorah,* by *R' Moshe Cordovero,* generally known as *RaMaK,* one of the most profound and systematic teachers of the *Zohar,* and a leading figure in the circle of mystics who assembled in sixteenth century Safed. Even the renowned *ARIzal, R' Isaac Luria,* refers to *RaMaK* as his teacher and master.

Since the Thirteen Attributes are meant to be emulated by man — rather than merely recited — *Tomer Devorah* takes pains to show how man can follow the example set by God in each of the attributes.

סדר תשליך

Tashlich Service

יהוה יהוה אל

רחום

[א] °מִי אֵל כָּמוֹךָ [ב] נֹשֵׂא עָוֹן [ג] וְעֹבֵר

וחנון   ארך

עַל פֶּשַׁע [ד] לִשְׁאֵרִית נַחֲלָתוֹ

◾§On the afternoon of the first day of Rosh HaShanah [or on the second day when the first day occurs on Shabbos] after Minchah services, it is customary to go to a river or body of running water — preferably containing live fish, or if impossible, even to a running wellspring — to recite *Tashlich*.

As noted in the commentary, the *Tashlich* service consists primarily of the recitation of verses from *Micah* 7:18—20: מִי אֵל כָּמוֹךָ וגו׳, which kabbalistically correspond to the Thirteen Divine Attributes in *Exodus* 34:6-7: ה׳ ה׳ אל רחום וגו׳; and of verses from *Psalms* 118:5—9: מִן הַמֵּצַר וגו׳, which correspond to the Nine Attributes in *Numbers* 14:18: ה׳ אֶרֶךְ אַפַּיִם וגו׳.

One should concentrate on the corresponding Attributes while reciting these verses, but should not articulate them *(ARIzal)*.

◾§ Attribute 1

מִי אֵל כָּמוֹךָ — *Who, O God, is like You?*
The translation follows *Malbim*. *Targum* paraphrases: There is no one but You, You alone are God. According to this rendering, the prophet directly addresses God and expresses his recognition that He is incomparable.

Others, however, do not designate אֵל as a Divine Name referring to God, but as a non-sacred word meaning *god* or *power*. *Who is a god like You?* Thus, the prophet tells God that nothing — idol, angel, or natural force — is like Him *(Ibn Ezra; Metzudas David)*.

Tomer Devorah explains that the Holy One, Blessed be He, is incomparable in His patience. To a degree beyond human understanding, he endures human behavior that, by its very nature, is insolent and insulting in the extreme. Consider that at every moment of man's existence, he is dependent on the Divine gifts of life and strength. It is man's responsibility to utilize these gifts in the service of God. Thus, when man sins against God, it is God's *own* strength that man turns against his Maker! Although this strength is used for sin, God does not withhold it from man, saying, 'If you choose to offend Me, you may not do so with the power I have granted you.' God is unlike any other power in the world: He patiently bears insult and sustains life that is used *against* Him — in the hope that man will repent.

Every man should emulate this Attribute by training himself to be patient, to bear insult, and even to bestow kindness upon those who abuse him.

◾§ Attribute 2

נֹשֵׂא עָוֹן — *Who pardons* [lit. *bears*] *iniquity.*

This attribute surpasses the preceding quality of patience, for an angel of destruction is created every time a man sins. *Avos* (4:11) teaches: He who commits a wrongdoing acquires a prosecutor for himself; this angel stands accusingly before the Holy One, Blessed be He, and says, 'That sinner created me.'

Who supplies the vital energy which allows this evil force to exist? God Himself! He could refuse to nourish the destructive angel, by saying, 'Go sap the life of the sinner who created you and exist on that.' Were this to happen, the sinner would be destroyed by the very nemesis he brought into being. But God

HASHEM, HASHEM,   GOD
[1] **W**ho, O God, is like You,
MERCIFUL
[2] **Who pardons iniquity**
AND COMPASSIONATE
[3] **And overlooks transgression**
SLOW
[4] **for the remnant of His heritage?**

is compassionate. He is נֹשֵׂא עָוֹן, literally, He *bears* or *carries iniquity*, [i.e., the destructive angel created by the sin]; He nourishes and sustains the evil force, so that the sinner may continue to live and have the opportunity to repent.

From this man should learn tolerance. Even when his neighbor offends him and even when the results of the offense are still in existence, the victim of wrongdoing should not harm his neighbor, but rather should wait patiently for the wrong to be righted.

⮜§ Attribute 3

וְעֹבֵר עַל פֶּשַׁע —*And overlooks* [lit. *passes over*] *transgression* [lit. *rebellion*].

It is God Himself Who grants forgiveness. He does not delegate this important function to a deputy or agent, as Scripture states: כִּי עִמְּךָ הַסְּלִיחָה, *For with You is the forgiveness* (Psalms 130:4). Furthermore, God Himself pours out clean water, as it were, to wash away the stains of sin. How shameful sin is, for the sinner obliges the Holy King *Himself* to cleanse his filthy garments!

This Attribute teaches man to be willing to rectify the damage caused by the sins of other men. Since every crime or perversion is an affront to God, man must strive to correct each offense, even if the act was not his own responsibility. Would we hesitate to save our neighbor's house from fire because we did not set the blaze?

⮜§ Attribute 4

לִשְׁאֵרִית נַחֲלָתוֹ — *For the remnant of His heritage.*

The word שְׁאָר means both *remnant* and *blood relative*. The prophet directs his words to the *remnant* of Israel who survived the long exile and who will receive special Divine kindness· (*Radak*).

God loves Israel as if the Jewish nation were a close relative. He calls her, 'My daughter,' 'My sister,' and 'My mother.' Thus, the Psalmist describes the Jews as בְּנֵי יִשְׂרָאֵל עַם קְרֹבוֹ, *The children of Israel, the nation related to Him* (Psalms 148:14).

God says, 'How can I punish Israel when her pain will be Mine?' The prophet states: *In all their sorrows He is afflicted* (Isaiah 63:9). God cannot bear Israel's pain or disgrace for it is His *remnant*, all that He has in His universe.

From God's love for us, a Jew learns how to love his fellow man. All Jews are related to each other; their souls are united, and in each soul there is a portion of all the others. For this reason, all Jews are responsible for one another (*Shavuos* 39a). Since each Jewish soul possesses a portion of all the others, when an Israelite sins, his wrong affects not only *his own* soul, but also the portion which all the others possess in him. It follows, therefore, that every Jew should love his neighbor as he loves himself, for he and his neighbor are one.

ורב־חסד אפים
[ה] לֹא הֶחֱזִיק לָעַד אַפּוֹ [ו] כִּי חָפֵץ חֶסֶד

נצר חסד ואמת
הוּא: [ז] יָשׁוּב יְרַחֲמֵנוּ [ח] יִכְבֹּשׁ עֲוֹנֹתֵינוּ

לאלפים
[ט] וְתַשְׁלִיךְ בִּמְצֻלוֹת יָם כָּל חַטֹּאתָם:

⋖§ Attribute 5

לֹא הֶחֱזִיק לָעַד אַפּוֹ — *Who has not retained His wrath eternally.*

The שְׁאָר, *remnant*, who endured the exile, are unworthy of redemption because they continue to be guilty of many of the shortcomings for which their fathers were first exiled. Nevertheless, God does not retain His wrath against them eternally (*Radak*).

This is another unique form of Divine mercy. Even when a man persists in sinning, God does not persist in retaining His anger. He allows His anger to abate even when man does not repent.

Man should employ this attribute when dealing with his neighbors. Even when he has the right to rebuke his neighbor, he should not persist in his rebuke nor continue his anger; he should end his wrath as soon as possible.

⋖§ Attribute 6

כִּי חָפֵץ חֶסֶד הוּא — *For He desires kindness.*

The Torah states, וְרַב חֶסֶד, *And He is abundant in kindness* (Exodus 34:6). When the time arrives for the redemption of Israel, God's kindness will overwhelm their sins (*Radak*).

Tomer Devorah comments that God has appointed special angels whose task is to gather in all the acts of kindness which Israel performs and to place them in a celestial treasury, as it were. When Israel's misconduct earns the accusations of the attribute of Strict Justice, these angels immediately bring Israel's kindness to the attention of the Almighty.

God delights in the acts of kindness which Jews perform for one another and remembers this aspect of their character even when they are guilty in other respects.

Man should imitate God's kindness. When he is hurt or provoked, let him look at the offender's good and admirable qualities (especially the quality of kindness to others). Then let him say, 'It is enough for me that he has shown kindness to another, or that he has some other fine trait.' Thus, He will delight in kindness.

⋖§ Attribute 7

יָשׁוּב יְרַחֲמֵנוּ — *He will again be merciful to us.*

Divine behavior differs from that of mortals. When a man has been offended, he cannot bring himself to love the one who offended him as much as he formerly did. But in the eyes of God, the repentant sinner enjoys a higher status than the man who has never sinned. As the *Talmud (Berachos* 34b) teaches: In the place and on the level where the penitent stands, the perfectly righteous cannot stand.

For those who have not sinned, a slight fence is sufficient to act as a barrier against sin. But such a barrier will not suffice for the penitent sinner. He must be very far removed from sin, lest the Evil Inclination tempt him again. Consequently, he must ascend higher and higher, closer and closer to God, in order to be shielded from further wrongdoing. Thus יָשׁוּב, *when he* [the penitent] *returns* to God, God's love will increase more and more, and יָשׁוּב יְרַחֲמֵנוּ, *God will return* [and reciprocate] and be even more *merciful to us.*

This is a guide for a man's behavior towards his neighbor. If his neighbor offended him but afterwards sought

[5] Who has not retained His wrath eternally,

AND ABUNDANT IN KINDNESS

[6] for He desires kindness!

AND TRUTH

[7] He will again be merciful to us;

PRESERVER OF KINDNESS

[8] He will suppress our iniquities.

FOR THOUSANDS OF GENERATIONS

[9] And cast into the depths of the sea

all their sins.

reconciliation, he should show him a greater degree of kindness than he did previously. He should encourage this neighbor even more than he would a perfectly righteous acquaintance who had never hurt him.

•§ Attribute 8

יְכְבּוֹשׁ עֲוֹנֹתֵינוּ — *He will suppress our iniquities.*

When a man fulfills a precept, he creates a powerful, flourishing force which grows until it enters God's celestial Presence. Sins, however, have no entry there, for God subdues and rejects them. The psalmist states: כִּי לֹא אֵל חָפֵץ רֶשַׁע אָתָּה לֹא יְגֻרְךָ רָע, *For You are not a god who desires wickedness, no evil sojourns with You* (Psalms 5:5).

Thus, there is no reward in This World for peforming a *mitzvah* (*Kiddushin* 39b), because the precept reaches God's heavenly Presence. The entire mundane world is not equal to the spiritual value of a single good deed. Furthermore, no limited earthly reward can compare to the infinite spiritual rewards of the World to Come.

God does not allow sins to cancel the effect of *mitzvos*. He does not say, 'Ten sins negate ten *mitzvos*,' so that the account is closed with neither punishment nor reward. *Mitzvos* are too precious to be cast aside so offhandedly. How can a sin, a mundane crime, cancel out a good deed which ascends to the highest heavens? God supresses our iniquities so that they do not rise before Him. Although the sins will be punished in

this lower world, the reward for *mitzvos* is reserved for the world of the spirit.

Similarly, a man should suppress the memory of any evil which was done to him, but remember every kindness. The good deeds should always be uppermost in his mind, so that he may sincerely appreciate them.

•§ Attribute 9

וְתַשְׁלִיךְ בִּמְצֻלוֹת יָם כָּל חַטֹאתָם — *And cast into the depths of the sea all their sins.*

It is from these words that the *Tashlich* ritual derives its name. This ninth attribute, as described by *Tomer Devorah*, demonstrates how man may actually shed his sins and cast them away.

Good men and evil deeds are an incongruous mixture. A Jew is innately good; his *essence* does not become evil despite his having sinned. Therefore, when a good man repents and purges himself of evil, the evil departs from him and returns to the spiritual depths, the realm of evil.

This is the secret of the Yom Kippur offering, of which it is written: *And the goat shall bear upon himself all of their iniquities and take them to a barren land* (Lev. 16:22).

The goat represents the forces of evil. Evil belongs to the forces of evil — to the barren wilderness — and not to Israel. When Israel sins, it, in effect, takes something — evil — which does not belong to it. When Israel repents, it

וְכָל חַטֹּאת עַמְּךָ בֵית יִשְׂרָאֵל תַּשְׁלִיךְ בִּמְקוֹם אֲשֶׁר לֹא יִזָּכְרוּ וְלֹא יִפָּקְדוּ
וְלֹא יַעֲלוּ עַל לֵב לְעוֹלָם.

ופשע

נשא עון

[י] תִּתֵּן אֱמֶת, לְיַעֲקֹב [יא] חֶסֶד לְאַבְרָהָם

ונקה

וחטאה

[יב] אֲשֶׁר נִשְׁבַּעְתָּ לַאֲבֹתֵינוּ [יג] מִימֵי קֶדֶם:

יהוה   ארך

[א] °מִן הַמֵּצַר, קָרָאתִי יָּהּ [ב] עֲנָנִי

---

sends the evil back to the source of evil, as if it is repaying a debt.

The wicked are likened to the raging sea, as the prophet said: *The wicked are like the troubled sea, for it cannot rest; its waters cast up mire and dirt* (Isaiah 57:20). Thus, the prophet Micah says, in effect, 'You will cast all of Israel's sins upon the wicked, who are likened to the muddy depths of the sea.'

A man can emulate this attribute. If he notices that his neighbor is crushed by suffering as a result of his sins, he should not disdain him for it. Rather, he should realize that suffering cleanses a man of sin and causes the evil to depart and to return to its source.

⋖§ Attribute 10

תִּתֵּן אֱמֶת לְיַעֲקֹב — *Grant truth to Jacob.*
Average, ordinary people who do not go beyond the letter of the law are called *Jacob*, for Jacob was a symbol of exact honesty. The name *Israel* is reserved for those who strive for extraordinary excellence.

God, too, possesses a quality of truth which follows the dictates of strict justice. Even for those who conduct themselves with precise truth as defined by the *halachah*, God exercises compassion, but only in accordance with His rigid standards of truth.

Every man should treat his neighbor with truth, and refuse to pervert Justice. Thus even the average man will be perfected in accordance with the quality of truth.

⋖§ Attribute 11

חֶסֶד לְאַבְרָהָם — *Kindness to Abraham.*
This refers to the righteous people who go beyond the letter of the law, as did the Patriarch Abraham. God reciprocates and behaves towards these people with *kindness* beyond the letter of the law.

When dealing with average men, a person should conduct himself with strict justice and truth. But when he comes in contact with those who are outstanding in their devotion to God, he should exceed the requirements of the law. If he is only slightly patient with ordinary men, he should strive to be exceptionally patient with the exceptionally devout. Such unique people should be exceedingly beloved to him.

⋖§ Attribute 12

אֲשֶׁר נִשְׁבַּעְתָּ לַאֲבוֹתֵנוּ — *As You swore to our fathers.*
The Holy One, Blessed be He, has mercy even upon the undeserving, because God swore to their forefathers that He would care for their descendants. In heaven, God has a special storehouse of grace, as it were, reserved for those who are unworthy; they receive this grace as an unearned gift.

Similarly, when a man meets an evildoer, he should not spurn him. Rather he should be gracious, saying, 'No matter what this man does, he remains the son of Abraham, Isaac, and Jacob. Even if he is unworthy, his forefathers were worthy. He who brings

[Some *Siddurim* add]: *And all the sins of Your nation, the House of Israel, cast away to a place where they will neither be remembered, considered, nor brought to mind — ever.*

FORGIVER OF INIQUITY

[10] **Grant truth to Jacob,**

TRANSGRESSION

[11] **kindness to Abraham,**

AND SIN

[12] **As You swore to our fathers**

ONE WHO ERASES

[13] **from ancient times** [*Micah* 7:18-20].

HASHEM,   SLOW

[1] **In distress I called upon YAH,**

TO ANGER

[2] **With abounding relief**

disgrace upon the children brings disgrace upon the fathers, and I have no desire to have the holy Patriarchs humiliated through me.'

◆§ Attribute 13

מִימֵי קֶדֶם — *From ancient times.*

If the merit of the forefathers is ever exhausted [see *Shabbos* 55a and *Tosafos, s.v.* וּשְׁמוּאֵל] and Israel is unworthy, what will God do? Israel has its *own* merit. It is written: זָכַרְתִּי לָךְ חֶסֶד נְעוּרַיִךְ, אַהֲבַת כְּלוּלֹתָיִךְ, לֶכְתֵּךְ אַחֲרַי בַּמִּדְבָּר, *I remember in your favor the kindness of your youth, your love as a bride when you followed after Me into the wilderness* (*Jeremiah* 2:2). God recalls all the good deeds which Israel performed from the day of its inception and He will relate to it with all His merciful attributes.

A man should conduct himself in similar fashion when he encounters a person who seems to be totally devoid of any redeeming virtue. He should say, 'Surely there was a time when this man had not yet sinned. Surely, in his early youth, while he was still uncorrupted, he performed some good deeds.' Using this attribute, no man will be found unworthy of goodness and mercy.

These are the Thirteen Attributes by which man can imitate the Creator. If man emulates these attributes on earth, he will trigger the higher Attribute of Mercy from above, and cause the Divine quality of mercy to shine upon the world. Therefore, repeat and remember these attributes, exhorts *Tomer Devorah*, so that they may be a constant reminder to follow in God's ways.

◆§ According to *Kabbalah*, Moses invoked nine attributes when he pleaded with God not to destroy Israel for its acceptance of the evil report of the מְרַגְּלִים, spies. These correspond to the nine attributes which the Kabbalists perceived in the selection from Psalms which follows. Again, the accounting of the Attributes follows the opinion of the *ARIzal*, and the Attributes derived from the Torah are written above those from the *Psalms*.

◆§ Attribute 1

מִן הַמֵּצַר קָרָאתִי יָּה — *In distress I called upon YAH.*
[This selection from *Psalms* reflects

the theme of *Rosh HaShanah*. Its first verse is also recited to introduce the blowing of the *shofar*. As the threat of harsh Divine judgment looms over the Jew on *Rosh HaShanah*, he is indeed in

בַּמֶּרְחַבְיָה: [ג] יהוה לִי [ד] לֹא אִירָא [ה] מַה

ופשע   ונקה

יַעֲשֶׂה לִי אָדָם: [ו] יהוה לִי בְּעֹזְרָי [ז] וַאֲנִי

לא ינקה   פקד עון אבות על־בנים

אֶרְאֶה בְשֹׂנְאָי: [ח] טוֹב לַחֲסוֹת בַּיהוה

על־שלשים ועל־רבעים

מִבְּטֹחַ בָּאָדָם: [ט] טוֹב לַחֲסוֹת בַּיהוה

מִבְּטֹחַ בִּנְדִיבִים:

---

deep distress. But when he senses that sincere repentance has removed his heavy burden of sin, he knows that God has answered him.

This concept corresponds to the symbolic casting away of sin which is the theme of *Tashlich.*

Radak attributes these words to David who was hiding in narrow and distressing caves [מֵצַר from צַר, *constriction*] during his flight from Saul.

During that time of woe and *distress,* God did not reveal His full Presence to David. Therefore, David did not refer to God with His full Name, HASHEM, but with the partial Divine Name יָה, YAH. Eventually, YAH did answer David *with abounding relief,* despite the fact that the Divine Presence was in eclipse (*Alshich*).

Radak suggests that the verse can also be understood as the collective plea of the Jews in exile. *Abarbanel* adds that the Jews here recall the difficult days in the מֵצַר of מִצְרַיִם, *Egypt.* [מִצְרַיִם may be read as מְצָרִים, *limits; straits.*] Just as God responded at that time when we called out to Him, so does He respond whenever we plead before Him in distress.

◄§ Attribute 2

עֲנָנִי בַמֶּרְחַבְיָה — *With abounding relief, YAH answered me.*

[In *Psalms* 4:2 we read: בַּצָּר הִרְחַבְתָּ לִּי, *You have relieved me of my distress.* צָר, *distress,* literally means *a tight, constricted place,* and הִרְחַבְתָּ, *relieved,* literally means *widened, enlarged.*

David said to the Holy One, Blessed be He, 'Master of the Universe, whenever I was constricted by difficult circumstances, You provided an avenue of relief and set me free. When I was caught in the dilemma of Bath Sheba, You presented me with a wonderful son, Solomon. When I was embroiled in the distress of all Israel, You eased my burden and gave me permission to prepare for the construction of the Holy Temple' (*Yerushalmi, Taanis* 2:9).

This declaration is an eloquent expression of one of David's most cherished credos: Never be discouraged by the terrible burdens and pressures of life, for every frustrating, enfeebling situation is actually a Divinely ordained opportunity to overcome adversity by fully utilizing one's talents and abilities. Thus, every distress which threatens to limit or diminish an individual, can serve to broaden his scope and to enlarge his soul. (See *comm.* to ArtScroll *Tehillim, Psalms* 4:2.)]

◄§ Attributes 3-4

ה׳ לִי — *HASHEM is with me.*

לֹא אִירָא — *I do not fear.*

YAH answered me [in the past] with abounding relief despite the fact that His Name was incomplete and His power was partially hidden. Therefore, when the full Name of HASHEM is with me, I [certainly] have no fear (*Alshich*).

◄§ Attribute 5

מַה יַּעֲשֶׂה לִי אָדָם — *What can man do to*

YAH answered me.

ABUNDANT IN KINDNESS   BEARER OF INIQUITY

[3] HASHEM is with me, [4] I do not fear —

AND TRANSGRESSION

[5] what can man do to me?

HE ERASES

[6] HASHEM is for me, through my helpers,

AND HE DOES NOT ERASE

[7] so I shall see the downfall

of my enemies.

HE ACCOUNTS THE INIQUITY OF THE FATHERS

[8] It is better to take refuge in HASHEM

than to rely on man.

TO THE THIRD GENERATION AND THE FOURTH GENERATION

[9] It is better to take refuge in HASHEM

than to rely on nobles [Psalms 118:5-9].

me? [Alternatively: *How can man affect me?*]

No individual can harm me *(Radak)*. Even an entire nation cannot overwhelm me or tear me from my faith *(Sforno)*.

[Man derives all his strength from God. If God has not ordained my death, how can my adversary destroy me?]

Abraham asked, 'What can my enemy Abimelech do to me?

Jacob asked, 'What can my malicious brother Esau do to me?'

David asked, 'What can my gigantic rival Goliath do to me?'

This may be compared to the King's favored attendant who was envied by the other courtiers. When they grew jealous and threatened his life, the favorite merely said, 'The king loves me and protects me. What, then, can the others do to me?' *(Midrash Shocher Tov).*

⧫§ Attribute 6

ה' לִי בְּעֹזְרָי — *HASHEM is for me, through my helpers* [lit. *HASHEM is with me, among my helpers*].

I have many helpers, but I place confidence in them *only* because HASHEM

is with them. If my helpers were not granted strength by God, their assistance would be futile and worthless *(Ibn Ezra).*

R' Vidal HaTzorfati and *Chasam Sofer* explain that although man can protect himself from his known enemies (*I shall see the downfall of my enemies*), he is still vulnerable to attack by those adversaries who pose as friends. Therefore the psalmist asks ה' לִי, *HASHEM be for me,* בְּעֹזְרָי, *for my* [ostensible] *helpers,* i.e., save me from false and treacherous friends.

⧫§ Attribute 7

וַאֲנִי אֶרְאֶה בְשֹׂנְאָי — *So I shall see [the downfall of] my enemies.* [Alt.: *Therefore I can face my foes.*]

Radak notes that the psalmist says something similar in *Psalms 54:9: From every distress He has rescued me, and upon my foes my eye has looked.*

The Sages teach that a person who *deserves* salvation is granted the privilege of witnessing the downfall of his enemies, as when Israel saw the death of the Egyptians at the Sea. However, he who is saved by the merits of others does not deserve this privilege. There-

רַנְּנוּ צַדִּיקִים בַּיהוה. לַיְשָׁרִים נָאוָה תְהִלָּה: הוֹדוּ
לַיהוה בְּכִנּוֹר. בְּנֵבֶל עָשׂוֹר זַמְּרוּ־לוֹ: שִׁירוּ־לוֹ
שִׁיר חָדָשׁ. הֵיטִיבוּ נַגֵּן בִּתְרוּעָה: כִּי־יָשָׁר דְּבַר־יהוה.
וְכָל־מַעֲשֵׂהוּ בֶּאֱמוּנָה: אֹהֵב צְדָקָה וּמִשְׁפָּט. חֶסֶד
יהוה מָלְאָה הָאָרֶץ: בִּדְבַר יהוה שָׁמַיִם נַעֲשׂוּ. וּבְרוּחַ
פִּיו כָּל־צְבָאָם: כֹּנֵס כַּנֵּד מֵי הַיָּם. נֹתֵן בְּאוֹצָרוֹת
תְּהוֹמוֹת: יִירְאוּ מֵיהוה כָּל־הָאָרֶץ. מִמֶּנּוּ יָגוּרוּ כָּל־
יֹשְׁבֵי תֵבֵל: כִּי הוּא אָמַר וַיֶּהִי. הוּא־צִוָּה וַיַּעֲמֹד: יהוה
הֵפִיר עֲצַת־גּוֹיִם. הֵנִיא מַחְשְׁבוֹת עַמִּים: עֲצַת יהוה
לְעוֹלָם תַּעֲמֹד. מַחְשְׁבוֹת לִבּוֹ לְדֹר וָדֹר: אַשְׁרֵי הַגּוֹי
אֲשֶׁר־יהוה אֱלֹהָיו. הָעָם בָּחַר לְנַחֲלָה לוֹ: מִשָּׁמַיִם
הִבִּיט יהוה. רָאָה אֶת־כָּל־בְּנֵי הָאָדָם: מִמְּכוֹן־שִׁבְתּוֹ
הִשְׁגִּיחַ. אֶל כָּל־יֹשְׁבֵי הָאָרֶץ: הַיֹּצֵר יַחַד לִבָּם. הַמֵּבִין
אֶל־כָּל־מַעֲשֵׂיהֶם: אֵין־הַמֶּלֶךְ נוֹשָׁע בְּרָב־חָיִל. גִּבּוֹר
לֹא־יִנָּצֵל בְּרָב־כֹּחַ: שֶׁקֶר הַסּוּס לִתְשׁוּעָה. וּבְרֹב חֵילוֹ
לֹא יְמַלֵּט: הִנֵּה עֵין יהוה אֶל־יְרֵאָיו. לַמְיַחֲלִים
לְחַסְדּוֹ: לְהַצִּיל מִמָּוֶת נַפְשָׁם. וּלְחַיּוֹתָם בָּרָעָב: נַפְשֵׁנוּ
חִכְּתָה לַיהוה. עֶזְרֵנוּ וּמָגִנֵּנוּ הוּא: כִּי־בוֹ יִשְׂמַח לִבֵּנוּ.
כִּי בְשֵׁם קָדְשׁוֹ בָטָחְנוּ: יְהִי־חַסְדְּךָ יהוה עָלֵינוּ. כַּאֲשֶׁר
יִחַלְנוּ לָךְ:

fore, Lot, who was saved by virtue of Abraham's merit was forbidden to look back upon the destruction of Sodom. Here the psalmist expresses confidence that he will be righteous enough to witness his enemies' defeat (Navah Tehillah).

R' Yoseif Leib Bloch of Telshe interprets the verse homiletically: It is a common maxim that a person is known through his enemies. If his enemies are righteous people, then he must be at fault, but if he is hated by the wicked, then he must be virtuous. The psalmist expresses his confidence that God will be among his helpers because *I see my enemies*, i.e., since my enemies are the wicked who defy God, I am sure that I am virtuous and worthy of His help. [See *The Haggadah Treasury*.]

◄§ Attribute 8

טוֹב לַחֲסוֹת בַּה׳ מִבְּטֹחַ בָּאָדָם — *It is better to take refuge in HASHEM than to rely on man.*

Rabbeinu Bachya and *Vilna Gaon*, explain the difference between the two closely related words חָסָיוֹן, *taking refuge*, and בִּטָחוֹן, *reliance*. The former denotes absolute confidence, even though no guarantees have been given. The latter presupposes a promise of protection, such as a pledge given by a powerful military or political figure.

The psalmist says that it is far better to trust in God's protection [even if God has made no explicit commitment] than to rely on the most generous assurance of any mortal. [See *Haggadah Treasury*.]

Sing joyfully, O righteous, because of HASHEM; for the upright, praise is fitting. Thank HASHEM with the Kinor, with the Neivel Ossor sing to Him. Sing Him a new song, play well with sounds of deepest feeling. For upright is the word of HASHEM, and His every deed is done with trust. He loves charity and justice, the kindness of HASHEM fills the earth. By the word of HASHEM the heavens were made, and by the breath of His mouth all their host. He assembles like a mound the waters of the sea, He places in vaults the deep waters. Fear HASHEM, all the earth; of Him be in dread, all inhabitants of the world. For He spoke and it became, He commanded and it stood firm. HASHEM annuls the counsel of peoples, He balks the designs of nations. But the counsel of HASHEM stands forever, the designs of His heart for all generations. Praiseworthy is the people whose God is HASHEM, the nation He chose for His own heritage. From heaven HASHEM looks down, seeing all of mankind. From His dwelling-place He oversees all inhabitants of earth, He Who fashions their hearts all together, Who comprehends all their deeds. A king is not saved by a great army, nor is a hero rescued by great strength; a sham is the horse, for salvation; despite its great strength, it provides no escape. Behold, the eye of HASHEM is on those who fear Him, upon those who await His kindness, to rescue from death their soul, and sustain them in famine. Our soul longed for HASHEM — our help and our shield is He. For in Him will our hearts be glad, for in His Holy Name we trusted. May Your kindness, HASHEM, be upon us, just as we awaited You [Psalm 33].

Radak cites the words of the prophet (Jeremiah 17:5): *Cursed be the person who relies on man and makes mortal flesh his supporting arm.* Even if circumstances do force a person to rely on his fellow man, he should place his main confidence in God, for it is He Who implants the desire to help in the heart of the human benefactor.

◆§ Attribute 9

טוֹב לַחֲסוֹת בַּה' מִבְּטֹחַ בִּנְדִיבִים — *It is better to take refuge in HASHEM than to rely on nobles.*

Ibn Ezra identifies the נְדִיבִים as the dignitaries whose prestige surpasses that of all other men.

Ibn Yachya determines that the נְדִיבִים are the seventy ministering angels, who are God's agents for governing the seventy peoples of the earth.

These seventy angels compose the heavenly tribunal which surrounds God's celestial throne. Those who are positioned on God's left are harsh and unrelenting in their demands for strict justice, whereas those who stand at God's right are נְדִיבִים [lit. *generous*] in their desire to treat mankind with compassion.

Nevertheless, it is far better *to take refuge in the mercy of HASHEM than to rely on* [the kindness of these] *noble angels* (Mahari Giktalia).

◆§ רַנְּנוּ צַדִּיקִים — Sing joyfully, O righteous.

[For commentary to this psalm, see ArtScroll *Tehillim* vol. II, psalm 33.]

לֹא־יָרֵ֥עוּ וְלֹֽא־יַשְׁחִ֖יתוּ בְּכָל־הַ֣ר קָדְשִׁ֑י, כִּֽי־מָלְאָ֣ה הָאָ֗רֶץ דֵּעָה֙ אֶת־יהוה, כַּמַּ֖יִם לַיָּ֥ם מְכַסִּֽים:

&8234;לֹא יָרֵעוּ — **They shall neither injure**
[lit. *they accomplish no evil*].

Malbim differentiates between the
terms מֵרִיעַ and מַשְׁחִית, both of which
refer to one who causes injury. The
מֵרִיעַ is *one who injures* for his own
benefit or pleasure, but the מַשְׁחִית is
one who destroys and gains nothing
from the damage he inflicts. The latter is
driven solely by the desire to destroy.

[The prophet foretells an era of tranquility and peace. Then harmony and
brotherhood will reign and even the
most hostile and malicious creature will
be tame and amiable.]

Prior to this, the prophet foretold:
*The wolf shall dwell with the sheep, the
leopard shall lay down with the kid, and
the calf, lion and cub and fatted cow
will be together (Isaiah 11:6).*

Radak explains that in the Messianic
era carnivorous animals will revert to
the herbivorous diet which they had
maintained before Adam's sin.

Leviticus 26:6 contains the Divine
promise, *And I will eradicate the evil
beasts from the earth.* *Ramban* quotes
two opinions cited in the *Midrash*: R'
Yehuda interprets this verse literally
and contends that the wild beast will actually be wiped out; R' Shimon,
however, maintains that only the *hostile
nature* of these creatures will disappear.

Ramban prefers the second opinion;
he explains that there were no predators
in the world before Adam sinned. Only
after man introduced evil into the world
did evil become ingrained into the
nature of certain beasts.

וְלֹא יַשְׁחִיתוּ — *Nor destroy.*
In the preceding verse (11:8), Isaiah
foresees a dramatic transformation in
the behavior of the most vicious
creatures: *The suckling babe shall play
on the scorpion's pit, and the weaned
child shall place his hand over the
viper's nest.* Ordinarily snakes are
מַשְׁחִית, they *destroy* without deriving
any pleasure from their prey. This
vicious, lethal urge will be tamed in the
epoch of the Messiah (*Malbim*).

בְּכָל הַר קָדְשִׁי — *In all of My sacred
mount.*

The mishnah (*Avos* 5:7) relates that
ten miracles were wrought for our
forefathers in the Temple. One of these
miracles was that a serpent or scorpion
never injured anyone in Jerusalem.

Tosefos Yom Tov observes that the
mishnah does not say that no snake ever
bit anyone in Jerusalem. That would not
necessarily indicate miraculous protection, for perhaps everyone took precau-
tions to stay a safe distance from these
deadly creatures. He explains that the
miracle was that even though people *did*
suffer occasional snake bites in Jerusalem, no one ever died as a result of these
injuries.

Midrash Shmuel and *Tiferes Yisrael*
(*Avos* 5:7) note that this phenomenon
persists to this very day. Although the
Temple lies in ruins the sanctity of the
Temple endures and counteracts the
poison of the snakes.

Based on this, we can explain the
words of Isaiah. In the past, the scor-
pions could not *kill* on the Temple
Mount, but they could bite and injure.
In the future, however, *they shall not
injure nor destroy* in any way at all.

The benign, sacred atmosphere which
emanates from *all the Holy Mount* will
spread throughout the world. The
predominance of sanctity will generate
an absence of sin, as the *Talmud*
(*Berachos* 33a) states: It is not the serpent, but man's sin which causes death.

> They shall neither injure nor destroy in all of My
> sacred mount, for the earth shall be filled with
> knowledge of HASHEM, as water covers the sea [Isaiah
> 11:9].

[The serpent is a symbol of sin because the very first creature to sin in the Garden of Eden was the serpent.]

כִּי מָלְאָה הָאָרֶץ דֵּעָה אֶת ה' כַּמַּיִם לַיָּם מְכַסִּים — *For the earth shall be filled with knowledge of HASHEM, as water covers the sea.*

Just as the sea is filled with water, the earth will be filled with the knowledge of God *(Metzudas David).*

At that time, God's Presence will be so apparent that even the wild beasts of prey will recognize Him. Even the dark and dumb earthiness of their nature will not obscure the infinite light of God's presence, just as nothing can restrain the power of the surging sea *(Malbim).*

Rambam (Hilchos Melachim 12:5) describes the future era of Messiah thus: At that time good things will be found in abundance; all luxuries will be as commonplace and available as dirt. Mankind will have no business nor concern other than the pursuit of the knowledge of God. Therefore, the Jewish people will be great sages who will comprehend matters hitherto regarded as incomprehensible. They will perceive the Divine intellect of their Creator, each and every one of them according to his own ability. As Scripture states, *the earth shall be full of the knowledge of HASHEM as waters cover the sea.* [Compare with *Rambam, Hilchos Teshuvah* 9:2].

Ohr Sameach (Hilchos Teshuvah 9:2) notes that *Rambam* emphasizes that everyone will perceive Divine intellect *according to his own ability.* In This World, people often fail in their pursuit of wisdom because they study either beneath or above their levels. Their learning is impeded because it does not correspond to their actual capacity. In the future, however, everyone will learn according to his own ability.

This may be likened to the water which covers the sea floor with utmost precision. Every available space is filled with water, and the sea holds its full volume of water *according to its ability.*

R' Avraham Yitzchak Bloch, quotes *Rambam (Hilchos Melochim* 12:1), who stresses that everything which happens in This World will continue in the future Messianic world; no extraordinary miracles will occur, no supernatural events will take place. If so, in what way will the future world be an improvement over the present one?

Actually, all 'natural' events are wondrous Divine accomplishments. However, since they occur according to a predictable pattern, man fails to appreciate that these 'natural' phenomena are Divine works. In the future, the processes of nature will not change; rather, a spirit of Divine wisdom will inspire man to perceive the Divine inner power which controls the world.

In this way, the future wisdom resembles the waters of the sea. The *Talmud (Chullin* 127a) states: Everything which is found on dry land can be found in the sea. The only reason that the marvels of the sea are not apparent to man is because they are covered by the waters. Similarly, the wonders of creation are not evident now because they are 'cloaked,' by the laws of nature, but Divine wisdom will reveal them all in the future.

לְדָוִד מִזְמוֹר לַיהוה הָאָרֶץ וּמְלוֹאָהּ. תֵּבֵל וְיֹשְׁבֵי
בָהּ: כִּי־הוּא עַל־יַמִּים יְסָדָהּ. וְעַל־נְהָרוֹת
יְכוֹנְנֶהָ: מִי־יַעֲלֶה בְהַר־יהוה. וּמִי־יָקוּם בִּמְקוֹם
קָדְשׁוֹ: נְקִי כַפַּיִם וּבַר־לֵבָב אֲשֶׁר לֹא־נָשָׂא לַשָּׁוְא
נַפְשִׁי. וְלֹא נִשְׁבַּע לְמִרְמָה: יִשָּׂא בְרָכָה מֵאֵת יהוה.
וּצְדָקָה מֵאֱלֹהֵי יִשְׁעוֹ: זֶה דּוֹר דֹּרְשָׁו. מְבַקְשֵׁי פָנֶיךָ
יַעֲקֹב סֶלָה: שְׂאוּ שְׁעָרִים רָאשֵׁיכֶם וְהִנָּשְׂאוּ פִּתְחֵי
עוֹלָם. וְיָבוֹא מֶלֶךְ הַכָּבוֹד: מִי זֶה מֶלֶךְ הַכָּבוֹד יהוה
עִזּוּז וְגִבּוֹר. יהוה גִּבּוֹר מִלְחָמָה: שְׂאוּ שְׁעָרִים
רָאשֵׁיכֶם וּשְׂאוּ פִּתְחֵי עוֹלָם. וְיָבֹא מֶלֶךְ הַכָּבוֹד: מִי
הוּא זֶה מֶלֶךְ הַכָּבוֹד יהוה צְבָאוֹת הוּא מֶלֶךְ הַכָּבוֹד
סֶלָה:

יְהִי רָצוֹן מִלְּפָנֶיךָ יהוה אֱלֹהֵינוּ וֵאלֹהֵי אֲבוֹתֵינוּ, הָאֵל הַגָּדוֹל
הַגִּבּוֹר וְהַנּוֹרָא, שֶׁתִּתְמַלֵּא רַחֲמִים עָלֵינוּ לְמַעַנְךָ וּלְמַעַן
קְדֻשַּׁת הַמִּזְמוֹר הַזֶּה, וְהַשֵּׁמוֹת הַקְּדוֹשִׁים הַנִּזְכָּרִים בּוֹ, וּקְדֻשַּׁת
פְּסוּקָיו וְתֵיבוֹתָיו וְאוֹתִיּוֹתָיו וְטַעֲמָיו וּרְמָזָיו וְסוֹדוֹתָיו, וּקְדֻשַּׁת
הַשֵּׁם הַקָּדוֹשׁ הַיּוֹצֵא מִפָּסוּק, וַהֲרִיקֹתִי לָכֶם בְּרָכָה עַד בְּלִי דָי,
וּמִפָּסוּק, נְסָה עָלֵינוּ אוֹר פָּנֶיךָ יהוה.

ו& תפלה על הפרנסה / Prayer for Livelihood

Since the pursuit of a livelihood can lead to many sins (such as dishonesty and theft), it is fitting to pray for an honest source of livelihood during the *Tashlich* ritual, when the supplicant strives to divorce himself from his transgressions.

The inclusion of this prayer in the *Rosh HaShanah* ritual is most appropriate, for Judaism teaches that man does not *make* a living, rather he *takes* a living, i.e., he acquires the portion of sustenance which was Divinely ordained for him.[1]

ו& **לְדָוִד מִזְמוֹר — Of David—a song.**
[For commentary to this psalm, see ArtScroll *Tehillim* vol. 1, psalm 24.]

ו& **יְהִי רָצוֹן — May it be desirable.**

וַהֲרִיקֹתִי לָכֶם בְּרָכָה עַד בְּלִי דָי —*I will pour out for you limitless blessing.*
Earlier in the verse, the prophet says: *Bring all of the tithe to the storage house so that there will be provisions in my house and test me please in this manner, says HASHEM of Legions, If I will not open for you the windows of heaven ...*

The *Talmud* (*Taanis* 9a) explains that, in general, it is forbidden to test the Almighty, for the Torah (*Deut.* 6:16) states: *You shall not test HASHEM, Your God.* The only exception is the precept of tithing, in regard to which God has promised, 'Tithe so that you may prosper'. The Jew is encouraged to test God's pledge in order to witness the validity of this Divine guarantee.

The reward for the strong faith which spurs a person to part with his tithe

◄§ Prayer for Livelihood

Of David — a song. HASHEM's is the earth and its fullness, the inhabited land and those who dwell in it. For He founded it upon seas, and established it upon rivers. Who may ascend the mountain of HASHEM, and who may stand in the place of His sanctity? One with clean hands and pure heart, who has not sworn in vain by My soul nor has he taken an oath deceitfully. He will receive a blessing from HASHEM and just kindness from the God of his salvation. This is the generation of those who seek Him, those who strive for Your Presence — Jacob. Selah. Raise up your heads, O gates, and be uplifted, you everlasting entrances, So that the King of Glory may enter. Who is the King of Glory? — HASHEM, the mighty and strong, HASHEM, the strong in battle. Raise up your heads, O gates, and raise up, you everlasting entrances, So that the King of Glory may enter. Who then is the King of Glory? HASHEM, of Legions, He is the King of Glory. Selah! [Psalm 24].

May it be desirable before You, HASHEM our God and the God of our fathers; the God Who is great, strong, and awesome — that You be filled with mercy upon us for Your sake and for the sake of this psalm's sanctity, and the sacred Names mentioned in it, and the sanctity of its verses, letters, cantillations, implications, mysteries, and the sanctity of the Holy Name which emanates from the verse: I will pour out for you limitless blessing [Malachi 3:10]; and from the verse: Let the light of Your countenance shine upon us, HASHEM [Psalms 4:7].

money or produce is an unlimited flow of riches: *I will pour out blessing for you without limit.* The words עַד בְּלִי דָי literally mean, 'until there is not enough.' The *Talmud (Taanis* 9a) explicates: עַד שֶׁיִּבְלוּ שִׂפְתוֹתֵיכֶם מִלּוֹמַר ,,דַּי'' *until your lips wear out from saying, 'Enough'.*

נָסָה עָלֵינוּ אוֹר פָּנֶיךָ ה' — *Let the light of Your countenance shine upon us, HASHEM.*

1. A wealthy merchant once approached the *Chofetz Chaim* for a blessing for success in his business ventures. The *tzaddik*, responded, 'May it be the will of God that you should enjoy the money which was inscribed in your Heavenly ledger on Rosh HaShanah and was sealed therein on Yom Kippur.'

The rich man was disappointed, 'Who needs such a blessing, since God will assure this regardless?'

The *Chofetz Chaim* explained, 'To wish you *more* than was allotted on Rosh HaShanah and

וְכָתְבֵנוּ בְּסֵפֶר פַּרְנָסָה טוֹבָה וְכַלְכָּלָה, שָׁנָה זוֹ וְכָל שָׁנָה
וְשָׁנָה, לָנוּ וּלְכָל בְּנֵי בֵיתֵנוּ, כָּל יְמֵי חַיֵּינוּ, בְּמִלּוּי וּבְרֶוַח בְּהֶתֵּר
וְלֹא בְּאִסּוּר, בְּנַחַת וְלֹא בְּצַעַר, בְּשַׁלְוָה וְהַשְׁקֵט וָבֶטַח, בְּלִי
שׁוּם עַיִן הָרָע.

וּתְזַכֵּנוּ לַעֲסוֹק בַּעֲבוֹדַת הַקּוֹדֶשׁ בְּלִי שׁוּם טְרָדָה, וּתְפַרְנְסֵנוּ
פַּרְנָסָה שֶׁלֹּא תִהְיֶה בָּהּ בּוּשָׁה וּכְלִמָּה, וְלֹא נִצְטָרֵךְ לְמַתְּנַת
בָּשָׂר וָדָם, כִּי אִם מִיָּדְךָ הַמְּלֵאָה וְהָרְחָבָה.

וְתַצְלִיחֵנוּ וְתַרְוִיחֵנוּ בְּכָל לִמּוּדֵנוּ וּבְכָל מַעֲשֵׂה יָדֵינוּ
וַעֲסָקֵנוּ, וְיִהְיוּ בָתֵּנוּ מָלֵא בִּרְכַּת יהוה, וְנִשְׂבַּע לֶחֶם וְנִהְיֶה
טוֹבִים:

David composed this psalm as he fled from his rebellious son, Absalom. Absalom and his followers claimed that their revolt was motivated by righteous intentions, but David reveals that their true desire was to emulate the monarchy of the gentile rulers. Absalom incited the masses to jealousy by showing them the prosperity and the tranquility of the heathen nations.

This verse begins: רַבִּים אֹמְרִים מִי יַרְאֵנוּ טוֹב, many always say, 'Who will show us good?', i.e., 'Where is the king who will sustain Israel with the wealth and abundance of the gentiles?'

David pities those who envy the material success of the gentiles, for these Jews deprive themselves of the rich experiences of Judaism which fill the devout with serene satisfaction and place them above petty ambitions. David pleads that God grant these envious ones the warmth and illumination of His Presence: Let the light of Your countenance shine upon us, HASHEM.

The word נְסָה literally means lift up. This verb is derived from נֵס, flag, standard. David said to those who lost their Jewish pride, ''Raise up a new 'standard' for yourselves: the light of God's shining countenance!''

[See commentary to ArtScroll Tehillim 4:7.]

וְכָתְבֵנוּ בְּסֵפֶר פַּרְנָסָה טוֹבָה — Inscribe us in the book of good sustenance.

Once a person's annual fortunes are inscribed in this Divine ledger, no one can deprive him of his lot. Moreover, in this ledger is also recorded by what means a person will earn his livelihood.

וְכַלְכָּלָה — And provision.

It is possible for God to assure כַלְכָּלָה, provision, even without giving actual פַּרְנָסָה, sustenance or livelihood.

The psalmist says (Psalms 145:16), פּוֹתֵחַ אֶת יָדֶיךָ, You open Your hands, referring to the sustenance of the rich

Yom Kippur is impossible. But to pray that you enjoy your precise portion is indeed good fortune. Some men are motivated by greed and ambition to increase their wealth. Even two jobs are insufficient for them; they are not satisfied without these. And behold, they do manage to earn much more than was allotted them on Rosh HaShanah. But it is impossible for them to keep this extra money, because it was not Divinely ordained. They will find that their fortune has caused them sorrow, for they are condemned to suffer large, painful losses to rid them of every extra, unauthorized penny they earned!'

'Therefore', concluded the Chofetz Chaim, 'the best blessing is to earn exactly the amount determined at the beginning of the year, so as to enjoy every penny without the pain of the slightest financial loss!'

The Chofetz Chaim also said, 'When someone tells me that he is making a living but it wouldn't hurt if things were a little better, I ask him, ''How do you know that it wouldn't hurt?'' God surely has the power to give a man more money. If He does not, it is because having more money would make things worse!'

Inscribe us in the book of good sustenance and provision — this year and every single year — us and our entire household, all the days of our lives, with fullness and generosity, with license and not illegally, with ease and not with pain, with serenity, tranquility, and confidence; without the slightest evil eye.

Privilege us to engage in the sacred service free from any bother, and provide us a livelihood without inner shame or humiliation, so that we have no need for the gifts of flesh and blood, but only from Your hand — full and expansive.

Grant us success and achievement in all our studies and in our every handiwork and undertaking. May our homes be full of HASHEM's blessing, may our bread satisfy us and may we be good.

---

men who have all the food they need. וּמַשְׂבִּיעַ לְכָל חַי רָצוֹן, *And you satisfy all living creatures with good will,* referring to the sustenance of the poor who are contented by the feeling of God's good will towards them which keeps them satisfied despite their lack of food (*Mechilta D'Rabbi Shimon bar Yochai*).[1]

לָנוּ וּלְכָל בְּנֵי בֵיתֵנוּ — *Us and our entire household.*

R' Yerucham Levovitz (*Daas Chochmah U'Mussar* Vol. 1, Essay 68, p. 213) comments on the folk saying 'One father can support ten sons but ten sons cannot support one father', that God or-

dained that parents maintain their dependent sons, but it is not a natural thing for sons to support their father.

A father should never forget that he is no more than a conduit through which his children receive what God has provided for them from above. Some parents mistakenly imagine that if they did not have so many children they would be much wealthier. They look forward to the day when their sons will become financially independent and leave home. This is a terrible fallacy. We have never seen a poor man who became rich when his many children finally became independent. In fact, the more children one has, the greater the

---

1. The following is a vivid example of how God satisfies the needs of the poor without providing actual material sustenance:

מַשְׁלִיךְ קַרְחוֹ כְפִתִּים לִפְנֵי קָרָתוֹ מִי יַעֲמֹד, *He casts forth His ice like crumbs: Who can withstand His cold?* (Psalms 147:17).

Rashi quotes the *Midrash*, which renders פִתִּים as cognate with פַּת, *a piece of bread*, which signifies human sustenance. God sends forth His icy winds in accordance with each person's פַּת, *bread*, i.e., sustenance and income. *Rashi* notes that the measure of cold which descends upon every individual is in direct proportion to his means. Since the poor man lacks adequate winter clothing, God lessens the intensity of the cold wind which blows at him.

This is illustrated in the story of R' *Yechezkel Abramsky*, who was exiled to Siberia by the Communists because of his religious activities as Rabbi of Slutzk. Since the Rabbi was usually very sensitive to cold weather, he feared that Siberia would be the death of him. However, he gathered his strength and prayed to God:

'The Sages say (*Kesubos* 30a) that everything is in the hands of Heaven except for colds and fever, for a person is responsible for his own health. But, HASHEM, this responsibility can only exist when a person has the means to protect himself from the cold. In this frigid land, however, I have been deprived of basic human necessities and I am incapable of warming myself. Therefore, the responsibility to safeguard my health reverts to You, HASHEM!'

רַחוּם, חַנּוּן, שׁוֹמֵר, תּוֹמֵךְ, וּמַצִּיל, יָשָׁר, פּוֹדֶה, רַחֵם עָלֵינוּ,
וּשְׁמַע תְּפִלָּתֵנוּ, כִּי אַתָּה שׁוֹמֵעַ תְּפִלַּת כָּל פֶּה. בָּרוּךְ שׁוֹמֵעַ
תְּפִלָּה. יִהְיוּ לְרָצוֹן אִמְרֵי פִי וְהֶגְיוֹן לִבִּי לְפָנֶיךָ, יהוה צוּרִי
וְגֹאֲלִי.

ﬁ‎ תחינות ובקשות

The following additional supplications are traditionally recited at the *Tashlich*
service. They were composed by the famous scholar, kabbalist, and
bibliographer, The 'Chidah' — R' Yosef Chaim David Azulai (1724-1806).

אֵל מָלֵא רַחֲמִים, גָּלוּי וְיָדוּעַ לְפָנֶיךָ כִּי בוֹשְׁנוּ בְּמַעֲשֵׂינוּ
וְנִכְלַמְנוּ בַּעֲוֹנֵינוּ בְּהַעֲלוֹתֵנוּ עַל־לְבָבֵנוּ רוֹב
קְצוּרֵנוּ בַּעֲבוֹדָתֶךָ, וּבְעֶסֶק תּוֹרָתֶךָ, וְקִיּוּם מִצְוֹתֶיךָ. וְנָמֵס לְבָבֵנוּ
בְּקִרְבֵּנוּ וְהָיָה לְמָיִם.

מַה גֵּעֲנֶה וּמַה נֹּאמַר? כִּי הַצַּר הַצּוֹרֵר בְּחֶבְרַת הַחוֹמֶר
הָעָכוּר הָיוּ בְעוֹכְרֵנוּ! גַּם אָסוּר נִלְוֶה עִמָּם, אֲסוּרִים וּלְטוּשִׁים,
גָּלוּת הַנֶּפֶשׁ וְהַגּוּף.

---

flow of blessing from above. As the demands of the children diminish, the
flow from heaven also decreases.

כָּל יְמֵי חַיֵּינוּ — *All the days of our lives.*
The sum total of our annual income is
decided on *Rosh HaShanah*. It is usually doled out in small amounts
throughout the year, precisely when
needed.

A pauper once appeared before *Rava*, who
asked him what he was accustomed to eat.

The poor man replied, 'I usually dine on
stuffed plump chicken, and fine old wine.'

Rava was surprised by this and inquired,
'Are you not concerned lest your expensive
tastes prove to be a burden upon the community which supports you?'

The beggar retorted, 'Am I really eating
from the hands of the community? I am
eating from the hand of the All Merciful!
Have we not learned *The eyes of all look
hopefully to You, and You give them their
food in its due season (Psalms 145:15)?'*

ﬂ‎ תחינות ובקשות / Additional Supplications

In the following section, the supplicant bemoans the frailty of man who is beset
by a host of powerful lusts and overwhelming desires. *Mesillas Yesharim* (Chapter
1) describes the incessant struggle confronting man:

God placed man in the midst of a raging battle, because all of the affairs of this
world, whether for good or evil are trials to a man. Every life circumstance — wealth
or poverty, serenity or suffering — contains its own challenge. The fierce battle
rages against man to the fore and to the rear. If he is valorous and victorious on all
sides, he will emerge as the אָדָם הַשָּׁלֵם, *the complete man.*

Chovas Halevovos (Shaar Yichud HaMa'aseh 5) tells of the pious man who went
out to greet the troops returning from the battlefront. He said to them, 'You are
returning from a minor skirmish to enter into the major battle — man's lifelong
struggle against his Evil Inclination.'

ﬂ‎ אֵל מָלֵא רַחֲמִים — O God, full of
Mercy.

בּוֹשְׁנוּ בְּמַעֲשֵׂינוּ וְנִכְלַמְנוּ בַּעֲוֹנֵינוּ — *We are
shamed by our deeds and disgraced by*

O Merciful and Compassionate One! Guardian, Support, Rescuer, Just One, Redeemer! Have mercy on us and hear our prayer, for You hear the prayer of every mouth. Blessed be He Who hears prayers. May the expressions of my mouth and the thoughts of my heart find favor before You, HASHEM, my Rock and my Redeemer [Psalms 19:15].

◆§ Additional Supplications

God, full of Mercy, it is revealed and known before You that we are shamed by our deeds and disgraced by our iniquities when we bring to mind our abundant deficiency in Your service, in the involvement with Your Torah, and in the fulfillment of Your commandments. Our heart melts within us and becomes like water [see Isaiah 19:1, Hoshea 7:5].

What can we answer — what can we say? It is the ceaseless Tormentor accompanied by our sordid materialism that caused our besmirching! Also the forbidden joined with them — forbidden yet burnished — causing estrangement of soul and body.

our iniquities.

Malbim (comm. to *Psalms 35:4)* explains that בּוּשָׁה, *shame,* is a relatively mild, self-imposed form of embarrassment which occurs when a person recognizes the inadequacies of his own actions. However, בְּלִימָה, *disgrace,* is a more intense form of humiliation which occurs when others notice the iniquities of the sinner.

בְּהַעֲלוֹתֵנוּ עַל לְבָבֵנוּ רוֹב קִצּוּרֵנוּ בַּעֲבוֹדָתֶךְ וּבְעֵסֶק תּוֹרָתֶךְ וְקִיּוּם מִצְוֹתֶיךָ — *When we bring to mind our abundant deficiency in Your service, in the involvement with Your Torah, and in the fulfillment of Your commandments.*

Our debt to God is limitless, but we are woefully limited. How can we ever fully discharge our obligations to Him?

כִּי הַצַּר הַצּוֹרֵר — *It is the ceaseless Tormentor.*

The Evil Inclination is man's most powerful tormentor and adversary. The *Talmud (Kiddushin* 30b) observes that even God — Creator of the Evil Inclination — calls it *evil.* This desire renews its assault every day, attempting to overwhelm man and destroy him. If man did

not receive Divine assistance, he could not withstand these incessant attacks.

בְּחֶבְרַת הַחוֹמֶר הָעָכוּר הָיוּ בְּעוֹכְרֵנוּ — *Accompanied by our sordid materialism that caused our besmirching!*

On describing the trait of נְקִיּוּת, *cleanliness, Mesillas Yesharim* (ch. 10) alludes to the *filthy materialism* of which man strives to free himself. It is the trace of evil which lust leaves behind it. Such evil causes man to deceive himself and assign value to the empty temptations of material life.

גַּם אָסוּר נִלְוָה עִמָּם — *Also the forbidden joined with them.*

This is a play on words based on *Psalms* 83:9: גַּם אַשּׁוּר נִלְוָה עִמָּם, *even Assyria joined with them.*

The verse refers to the massive gentile host which gathered to destroy Israel; in the context of the *Tashlich* prayer, the phrase refers to the host of temptations that influence man to sin.

אֲסוּרִים וּלְטוּשִׁים — *Forbidden yet burnished* [i.e., *gleamingly tempting*].

This is a play on words based on *Genesis* 25:3, where the progeny of

אָמְנָם גָּלוּי וְיָדוּעַ לְפָנֶיךָ שֶׁרְצוֹנֵנוּ לַעֲשׂוֹת רְצוֹנֶךָ וְלִשְׁקוֹד
עַל דַּלְתוֹתֶיךָ, כִּי טוֹב יוֹם בַּחֲצֵרֶיךָ מֵאָלֶף בָּחַרְנוּ.
וִירֵאִים וַחֲרֵדִים אֲנַחְנוּ מֵאֵימַת דִּינֶךָ הַקָּדוֹשׁ. עַל כֵּן בָּאנוּ
אֵלֶיךָ בִּכְפִיפַת רֹאשׁ, וּנְמִיכַת קוֹמָה, וַחֲלִישׁוּת חָיִל, לְהַזְכִּיר
וּלְעוֹרֵר רַחֲמֶיךָ וּלְהַזְכִּיר זְכוּת אֲבוֹתֵינוּ הַקְּדוֹשִׁים, וּבִזְכוּתָם
תִּתְמַלֵּא רַחֲמִים עָלֵינוּ:

וִיהִי רָצוֹן מִלְּפָנֶיךָ יהוה אֱלֹהַי וֵאלֹהֵי אֲבוֹתַי, אֵל עֶלְיוֹן
מֻכְתָּר בִּתְלֵיסַר מְכִילִין דְּרַחֲמֵי, שֶׁתְּהֵא שָׁעָה
זוֹ עֵת רָצוֹן לְפָנֶיךָ. וְיִהְיֶה עוֹלֶה לְפָנֶיךָ קְרִיאַת שְׁלֹשׁ עֶשְׂרֵה
מִדּוֹת שֶׁל רַחֲמִים שֶׁבַּפְּסוּקִים, מִי אֵל כָּמוֹךָ (וגו'), הַמְכֻוָּנִים
אֶל שְׁלֹשׁ עֶשְׂרֵה מִדּוֹת, אֵל רַחוּם וְחַנּוּן (וגו'), אֲשֶׁר קָרִינוּ
לְפָנֶיךָ, כְּאִלּוּ הִשַּׂגְנוּ כָּל הַסּוֹדוֹת וְצֵרוּפֵי שְׁמוֹת הַקְּדוֹשִׁים

Abraham and Keturah are listed: וּבְנֵי דְּדָן הָיוּ אַשּׁוּרִם וּלְטוּשִׁם, *And the sons of Dedan were Ashurim and Letushim.*

In the context of this supplication, the word signifies that the Evil Inclination entices us to draw near to *proscribed* things which should be kept at a distance.

שֶׁרְצוֹנֵנוּ לַעֲשׂוֹת רְצוֹנֶךָ — *That it is our will to do Your will.*

At the conclusion of the *Shemoneh Esrei*, R' Alexandri would say 'Master of the Universe, it is clearly evident to You that our wish is to fulfill Your wish, but what inhibits us? The yeast in the dough [i.e. the Evil Inclination which 'sours' us just as yeast sours dough (*Rashi*)] (*Berachos* 17a).

וְלִשְׁקוֹד עַל דַּלְתוֹתֶיךָ — *And diligently to guard Your doorways.*

This is based on *Proverbs* 8:34, אַשְׁרֵי אָדָם שֹׁמֵעַ לִי לִשְׁקֹד עַל דַּלְתֹתַי יוֹם יוֹם, *Praiseworthy is the man who hearkens to Me to guard My doorways* [i.e., the entrances to the House of Study] *diligently, day after day.*

כִּי טוֹב יוֹם בַּחֲצֵרֶיךָ מֵאָלֶף בָּחַרְנוּ — *For better a day in Your courtyards than a thousand — that is our choice.*

This is based on *Psalms* 84:11.

It is far better to dwell in Your Presence [i.e., in the Temple] today and to die tomorrow than to live elsewhere [in exile] for one thousand years (*Targum; Rashi; Radak*).

[For in Your Presence, my spirit flourishes, but estranged from You, it withers.][1]

Indeed, even one day of life in This World surpasses all of the existence in the World to Come [*Avos* 4:17], for This World is a *courtyard*, where one prepares himself before entering the main hall, the World to Come [*Avos* 4:16]. Only in this world can man fulfill God's commandments and gain merits which will enrich his future reward. In the World to Come it is too late, for

1. The *Talmud* (*Makkos* 10a) relates that David said to the Holy One, Blessed be He, 'Sovereign of the Universe, I overheard people saying, 'When will this old man [i.e. David] die, so that his son Solomon may build the Temple and enable us to make the festival pilgrimage to that Holy Place?' David rejoiced when he heard this [because it demonstrated how intensely the people yearned to serve God].

But God was not pleased. He said, '*Far better a day in your courtyard than a thousand*', i.e., a single day of David's devoted Torah study in My Presence surpasses the one thousand burnt-offerings which Solomon is destined to sacrifice before me on the Temple altar. [See footnote to *Psalms* 39:5, which cites *Shabbos* 30a.]

However it is revealed and known before You that it is our will to do Your will [Berachos 17a] and diligently to guard Your doorways [Proverbs 8:34], for better a day in Your courtyards than a thousand — that is our choice [Psalms 84:11].

We are awestruck and terrified by the specter of Your sacred Judgment. We therefore come to You, with bowed heads, lowered statures, and exhausted strength, to summon and arouse Your mercy, and to recall the merit of our sacred forefathers. And in their merit be filled with mercy upon us.

May it be desirable before You, HASHEM, our God and the God of our fathers, most Exalted God crowned with thirteen tiaras of mercy, that this moment be propitious before You, and may You consider our recital of the Thirteen Attributes of Mercy which are alluded to in the verses beginning 'Who, O God, is like You... [Micah 7:18],' corresponding to the Thirteen Attributes in the verses of 'O God, Merciful and Compassionate [Exodus 34:6]', which we have read before You, as if we had comprehended all the mysteries and the combinations of the Holy Names which emanate from them and the union of the At-

---

there man can but reap the fruits of what he planted in This World (*Alshich; Meir Tehillos*).

וִירֵאִים וַחֲרֵדִים אֲנַחְנוּ מֵאֵימַת דִּינְךָ הַקָּדוֹשׁ — *We are awestruck and terrified by the specter of Your sacred Judgment.*

When R' Yochanan ben Zakkai was on his deathbed, his disciples visited him. As soon as he saw them he burst into tears. When they asked him why, he replied:

'Were I to be brought before a mortal king — who is here today but in the grave tomorrow, who may become angry with me, but whose anger is not everlasting, who may imprison me, but whose imprisonment is not forever, who may kill me, but who can kill only for this world; and who may be bribed — even then I would fear! But now I am led before the King of Kings, the Holy One, Blessed be He, who lives through all eternity,' [should I not tremble before this awesome judgment?] If He is angry at me, His anger is everlasting; if He imprisons me, it is imprisonment forever; if He kills someone, that person

is dead forever; and I can neither appease Him with words nor bribe Him with money. Morever, there are two paths before me — one leading to Paradise and one leading to Hell — and I know not through which I am to be led. Should I not weep?' (*Berachos 28b*).

◆§ וִיהִי רָצוֹן — **May it be desirable.**

וִיהְיֶה עוֹלֶה לְפָנֶיךָ... כְּאִלּוּ הִשַּׂגְנוּ כָּל הַסּוֹדוֹת וְצֵרוּפֵי שְׁמוֹת הַקְּדוֹשִׁים הַיּוֹצְאִים מֵהֶם — *May You consider* [lit. *may it ascend before You*]... *as if we had comprehended all of the mysteries and the combinations of the Holy Names which emanate from them.*

Ramban explains in his introduction to the Torah that the letters of the Torah can be divided to form different words than those to which we have become accustomed. By so doing, innumerable Names of God — both those known to us and His hidden, mystical ones — can be formed. Thus, when we read our text of the Torah, we are actually reading much more than the words we pronounce. We also read concealed

הַיּוֹצְאִים מֵהֶם, וְזִוּוּגֵי מִדּוֹתֵיהֶם אֲשֶׁר אֶחָד בְּאֶחָד יִגְּשׁוּ.
לְהַמְתִּיק הַדִּינִים תַּקִּיפִים וּבְכֵן, וְתַשְׁלִיךְ בִּמְצֻלוֹת יָם כָּל
חַטֹּאתֵינוּ.

וְאַתָּה בְּטוּבְךָ תְּעוֹרֵר רַחֲמֶיךָ וְנִהְיֶה נְקִיִּים מִכָּל טֻמְאָה
וְחֶלְאָה וְזוּהֲמָא, וְיַעֲלוּ כָּל נִיצוֹצוֹת הַקְּדוֹשָׁה אֲשֶׁר נִתְפַּזְּרוּ
וְיִתְבָּרְרוּ וְיִתְלַבְּנוּ בְּמִדַּת טוּבְךָ. אַתָּה אֵל יְשׁוּעָתֵנוּ נֹצֵר חֶסֶד
לָאֲלָפִים.

וּבְרֹב רַחֲמֶיךָ תִּתֶּן לָנוּ חַיִּים אֲרוּכִים, חַיִּים שֶׁל שָׁלוֹם, חַיִּים
שֶׁל טוֹבָה, חַיִּים שֶׁל בְּרָכָה, חַיִּים שֶׁל פַּרְנָסָה טוֹבָה, חַיִּים שֶׁל
חִלּוּץ עֲצָמוֹת, חַיִּים שֶׁיֵּשׁ בָּהֶם יִרְאַת חֵטְא, חַיִּים שֶׁאֵין בָּהֶם
בּוּשָׁה וּכְלִימָה, חַיִּים שֶׁל עוֹשֶׁר וְכָבוֹד, חַיִּים שֶׁתְּהֵא בָּנוּ

ideas and combinations of letters that form various Names of God.

וְזִוּוּגֵי מִדּוֹתֵיהֶם אֲשֶׁר אֶחָד בְּאֶחָד יִגְּשׁוּ — *And the union of these Attributes which converge upon one another.*

As explained above, the Thirteen Attributes listed in *Exodus* correspond to the Thirteen Attributes enumerated by the prophet Micah.

לְהַמְתִּיק הַדִּינִים תַּקִּיפִים — *May this sweeten the harsh Judgments.*

Even after the heavenly tribunal issues a sentence against the sinner, it is possible to 'soften' the blow.[1]

וְיַעֲלוּ כָּל נִיצוֹצוֹת הַקְּדוֹשָׁה אֲשֶׁר נִתְפַּזְּרוּ וְיִתְבָּרְרוּ וְיִתְלַבְּנוּ בְּמִדַּת טוּבְךָ — *May all the sacred sparks which were scattered ascend and be clarified and whitened through Your Attribute of Goodness.*

The purpose of every object, molecule, and atom, is to bring glory to God's Name. This potential to glorify God — the נִיצוֹץ קָדוֹשׁ, *holy spark* — rests concealed and dormant within an object until someone performs a meritorious action with it.

Even a profane article possesses the potential to sanctify God's Name and

challenges man to do so. If he is successful, he redeems the spark in this unclean object (*Michtav M'Eliyahu* Vol. II p. 255).

R' Chaim of Volozhin comments that the life-giving force of any food is the Divine spark within it. That spark emanates from God's utterance, *Let grain spring forth from the earth* (*Genesis* 1:11). When a person recites a blessing over his food, he releases the Divine spark, the spiritual energy hidden in the food. This holy force sustains life (*Ruach Chaim*).

וּבְרֹב רַחֲמֶיךָ תִּתֶּן לָנוּ חַיִּים אֲרוּכִים — *In Your abundant mercy, grant us long life.*

Beginning with this request for long life until the conclusion of this section, the supplication quotes verbatim from the prayer of Rav, the foremost Talmudic sage of his era. He was accustomed to recite it daily upon the conclusion of his daily prayer (*Berachos* 16b), and it has been adoped as part of the liturgy in the prayer for the new month.

A careful study of this supplication reveals that everything which Rav included here reflects his personal values and the events of his life.

1. On Rosh HaShanah and Yom Kippur mankind is judged and sentenced. The verdicts may sometimes be very harsh, but God still offers an opportunity for mercy. Immediately following these Days of Awe, the Jew is 'exiled' from his home into the *Succah*, because exile is a source of atonement for sin. If rain prevents him from entering the *Succah*, however, it is an indication that God refuses to allow him atonement for the verdict of the Days of Judgment. This is the allegorical deeper meaning of the mishnah (*Succah* 1:9) which speaks of a master who splashes water in the face of a servant who offers him wine (*Vilna Gaon*).

tributes which converge upon one another. May this sweeten the harsh Judgments and may You cast into the depths of the sea all our sins.

May You, in Your goodness, arouse Your mercy so that we may be cleansed of all contamination, filth, and defilement. May all the sacred sparks which were scattered ascend and be clarified and whitened through Your Attribute of Goodness. You, O God of salvation, who guards lovingkindness for two thousand generations.

In Your abundant mercy, grant us long life, a life of peace, a life of goodness, a blessed life, a prosperous life, a vigorous life, a life containing fear of sin, a life free of shame and humiliation,

חַיִּים שֶׁל שָׁלוֹם — *A life of peace.*

In his personal dealings, Rav pursued peace and harmony under all circumstances. The *Talmud (Yoma* 87a) relates that a certain butcher mistreated Rav and quarreled with him. When the eve of the Day of Atonement arrived, the butcher did not come to ask Rav for forgiveness. 'If he does not come to me, said Rav, then I shall go to him to ask forgiveness!' On the road, R' Huna met Rav and inquired of him, 'Where is the Master going?' 'I am going to appease that man,' Rav replied. 'The Master is on his way to kill the man,' remarked Rav Huna. [Knowing that the butcher would refuse Rav's overture, R' Huna was sure that he would be sorely punished.]

When Rav arrived at the shop, the butcher was cleaning the head of a cow. The butcher noticed Rav and said, 'Is that you? Go away, for I want no dealings with you!' When the butcher resumed cleaning the cow's head, a bone splinter flew up striking him in the head and killing him.

חַיִּים שֶׁל טוֹבָה — *A life of goodness.*

The 'good' life is the life in which a man has the opportunity to enjoy every gift which God bestows. As Rav taught, possessions are meant to be used wisely and properly; not to be hoarded for some future which may never come (*Eruvin* 54a).

חַיִּים שֶׁל פַּרְנָסָה טוֹבָה — *A prosperous life.*

A *good sustenance* does not mean one which provides riches; it means an independent livelihood which frees a man from envy of others and from dependence on them. Rav said, 'When a man yearns for the table [i.e., the provisions and livelihood] of another man, the world becomes dark for him (*Beitzah* 32b).

חַיִּים שֶׁל חִילוּץ עֲצָמוֹת — *A vigorous life* [lit. *a life of release of the bones*].

This blessing is based on the words of the prophet: וְעַצְמֹתֶיךָ יַחֲלִיץ וְהָיִיתָ כְּגַן רָוֶה, וּכְמוֹצָא מַיִם אֲשֶׁר לֹא יְכַזְּבוּ מֵימָיו, *And He will invigorate your bones, and you will be like a lush garden and a waterspring whose waters never cease to flow* (Isaiah 58:11).

The *Talmud (Yevamos* 102b) declares that one of the greatest blessings is robust health and vigor.

R' Yochanan testified that Rav came from a family well-known for its good health and strength (*Chullin* 84a).

חַיִּים שֶׁיֵּשׁ בָּהֶם יִרְאַת חֵטְא — *A life containing fear of sin.*

The text in *Berachos* 16b mentions only יִרְאַת חֵטְא, later the words יִרְאַת שָׁמַיִם were inserted. This addition teaches that genuine *fear of sin is based on fear of heaven.*

R' Avrohom Abba Kaplan explains that the more beloved an object, the greater the owner's fear lest it be damaged. Similarly, the more a person treasures *heaven* — i.e., God — the more

אַהֲבַת תּוֹרָה וְיִרְאַת חֵטְא, חַיִּים שֶׁתִּמָּלֵא כָל מִשְׁאֲלוֹת לִבֵּנוּ
לְטוֹבָה.

זָכְרֵנוּ לְחַיִּים, מֶלֶךְ חָפֵץ בַּחַיִּים, כָּתְבֵנוּ בְּסֵפֶר הַחַיִּים,
לְמַעַנְךָ אֱלֹהִים חַיִּים. וְקָרַע רוֹעַ גְּזַר דִּינֵנוּ, וְיִקָּרְאוּ לְפָנֶיךָ
זְכִיּוֹתֵינוּ.

אֵל מָלֵא רַחֲמִים, יֶהֱמוּ נָא רַחֲמֶיךָ עָלֵינוּ לְקַבֵּל בְּרָצוֹן
הַכְנָעָתֵנוּ וְהַרְהוֹרֵי תְשׁוּבָתֵנוּ הַמִּתְנוֹצְצִים בָּנוּ.
וּתְקַיֵּם לָנוּ מַה שֶּׁהִבְטַחְתָּנוּ עַל יְדֵי עֲבָדֶיךָ חַכְמֵי יִשְׂרָאֵל,
,,הַבָּא לְטַהֵר מְסַיְּעִין אוֹתוֹ".
וּבְשֶׁגַּם לִבֵּנוּ אָטוּם סָתוּם וְחָתוּם, וְלֹא אִתָּנוּ יוֹדֵעַ זוֹ הִיא
שִׁיבָה זוֹ הִיא בִיאָה, רַב לְהוֹשִׁיעַ, הָאֵר עֵינֵינוּ כַּאֲשֶׁר בְּגֹדֶל

---

he is afraid to sin, lest he ruin the special relationship he enjoys with God.

חַיִּים שֶׁל עוֹשֶׁר וְכָבוֹד — *A life of wealth and honor.*

The *Chofetz Chaim* asked, 'How can we request honor, since we know that רְדִיפַת הַכָּבוֹד, *the pursuit of honor and acclaim,* is a most despicable trait? We seek riches only in order to bring glory to the Jewish people as a whole, but not for ourselves. Similarly, in the liturgy of the High Holidays we pray, וּבְכֵן תֵּן כָּבוֹד ה' לְעַמֶּךָ, *And thus, grant honor, HASHEM, to Your nation.*

The *Talmud (Berachos 57b)* relates that Rav was a man of wealth. Rav knew that prosperity brings its possessor dignity and honor, yet, the rich man must take care not to become overly proud and arrogant.

Accordingly, we ask for *prosperity* coupled with the real *honor* which comes when a person's wealth and status are used properly in God's service, without resulting in vanity and arrogance.

In addition, the rich man should strive to bring *honor* to himself by giving charity with his riches. Rav said, 'The rich men of Babylonia will someday inherit an estate in Hell.' [This is because they lack mercy and give no charity (*Rashi*)] (*Beitzah* 32b).

חַיִּים שֶׁתְּהֵא בָּנוּ אַהֲבַת תּוֹרָה — *A life in which love of Torah... is within us.*

Rav's insatiable love of Torah is reflected in his statement: 'A person should never refrain from attending the House of Study even for a moment [lest, during his absence, he miss an important lesson] (*Shabbos* 83b).

A few phrases earlier, the wording is חַיִּים שֶׁיֵּשׁ בָּהֶם, *a life which holds...,* but now the prayer reads חַיִּים שֶׁתְּהֵא בָּנוּ, *a life in which it is within us.* First we ask for the externals —the outer lifestyle of the Jew. Now we request deeper meaning, inner commitment and sincerity. This can be accomplished only through love of Torah and its study.

וְיִרְאַת חֵטְא — *And fear of sin.*

In the standard liturgy of בִּרְכַּת הַחֹדֶשׁ, *the Blessing of the New Moon,* the text reads וְיִרְאַת שָׁמַיִם, *and fear of heaven.*

Actually, these words are a repetition of an earlier request for וְיִרְאַת חֵטְא. *Chofetz Chaim* explains that since we subsequently ask for a *life of prosperity and honor* — which can pose a grave threat to one's character by fostering arrogance and the defiance of God — a *second* plea for *fear of sin* is required.

חַיִּים שֶׁתִּמָּלֵא כָל מִשְׁאֲלוֹת לִבֵּנוּ לְטוֹבָה — *A life in which You favorably fulfill all the desires of our heart for goodness.*

a life of wealth and honor, a life in which love of Torah and fear of sin are within us, a life in which You favorably fulfill all the desires of our heart for goodness.

Remember us for life, O King Who desires life; inscribe us in the Book of Life, for Your sake, O Living God. Tear up the inauspicious verdict against us and may our merits be read before You.

O God, full of mercy, please let Your Mercy yearn for us, so that You may graciously accept our submission and our penitential reflections which sparkle within us. May You fulfill Your assurance given us through Your servants, the Sages of Israel: 'Whoever strives for purity is divinely assisted.'

Inasmuch as our heart is blocked, closed and sealed — none among us knowing how to return to You or how to approach You; therefore, You Who saves magnanimously, set our eyes

Not always are a man's desires truly in his best interest; he may very well yearn for something harmful. Therefore, upon completing this list of requests, we ask that they be fulfilled in a manner which is not detrimental (*Rashash* to *Berachos* 16b).

אֵל מָלֵא רַחֲמִים — O God full of Mercy.

This supplication captures the humility and submissiveness of a people eternally loyal and devoted to the Creator. Israel is helpless without God's assitance, but it recognizes that it is unworthy of His aid. Israel claims for itself only one merit: throughout the millennia, millions of its sons and daughters have martyred themselves to sanctify His Name. Israel asks God to grant His people the opportunity to consecrate God's Name in life rather than in death.

הַבָּא לְטַהֵר מְסַיְּעִין אֹתוֹ — Whoever strives for purity is divinely assisted.

R' Simchah Zissel Ziev of Kelm illustrates this concept with a parable. A king once promised a great reward to anyone who could scale a ladder of a hundred rungs. People were attracted from far and wide — but when they saw the ladder, they left without even making the attempt — the task was impossible. One man felt otherwise. Would his

king have asked for the impossible? No — it *could* be done, and he set himself to try. He began to climb, but before he had reached even the tenth rung, he was exhausted and about to fall. As he gathered enough strength to scale the tenth rung, he felt himself lifted, as if by a huge magnet, and placed atop the ladder. Indeed, the royal wish was not that the impossible be accomplished, but that man exert himself to the limit of his ability. So it is with our spiritual quest. God wants us to scale great spiritual heights, but He knows we cannot do it alone. If we make the effort — sincerely, diligently, uncompromisingly — He gives us His assistance, without which success is impossible (heard from *Harav Mordechai Gifter*). [See Overview to ArtScroll *Jonah: Jonah, Repentance, and Yom Kippur* (p. xlviii).]

זוֹ הִיא שִׁיבָה זוֹ הִיא בִּיאָה — How to return to You or how to approach You.

This Talmudic phrase [found in *Eruvim* 51a; *Niddah* 22b] is based on *Leviticus* 14:39, 44, which speaks of the priest who checks the leprous sign on the stones of a house.

Scripture here implies that one needs an expert to scrutinize a sign of sin and defilement; but we, in our degradation, lack an expert who can reveal to us where our faults lie.

רַחֲמֶיךָ הִבְטַחְתָּנוּ: "פִּתְחוּ לִי פֶּתַח כְּחוּדוֹ שֶׁל מַחַט, וַאֲנִי אֶפְתַּח לָכֶם פֶּתַח כְּפִתְחוֹ שֶׁל אוּלָם".

וּרְאֵה כִּי אָזְלַת יָד וְאֶפֶס עָצוּר וְעָזוּב וְאֵין חוֹנֵן וְאֵין מְרַחֵם זוּלָתֶךָ כִּי חַנּוּנֶיךָ הֵמָּה חֲנוּנִים וּמְרוּחָמֶיךָ הֵמָּה מְרוּחָמִים. כְּדִכְתִיב: וְחַנֹּתִי אֶת־אֲשֶׁר אָחֹן, וְרִחַמְתִּי אֶת־אֲשֶׁר אֲרַחֵם. וּבְכֵן לֵב טָהוֹר בְּרָא לָנוּ אֱלֹהֵינוּ, וְרוּחַ נָכוֹן חַדֵּשׁ בְּקִרְבֵּנוּ.

וְרִשְׁפֵּי הִתְעוֹרְרוֹת לִבֵּנוּ בְּאַהֲבָתֶךָ וְתוֹרָתֶךָ יַתְמִידוּ וְיִתְרַבּוּ בְּלִי הֶפְסֵק. עָזְרֵנוּ אֱלֹהֵי יִשְׁעֵנוּ עַל דְּבַר כְּבוֹד שְׁמֶךָ.

תָּחֵל שָׁנָה וּבִרְכוֹתֶיהָ, וְתַצִּילֵנוּ מִשֶּׁבִי, וּמִבִּזָּה, וּמִכַּף כָּל אוֹיֵב וְאוֹרֵב וְשׁוֹלֵל וּבוֹזֵז, וְהָפֵר עֲצָתָם וְתִקְלְקֵל מַחְשְׁבֹתָם. תִּפּוֹל עֲלֵיהֶם אֵימָתָה וָפַחַד, בִּגְדוֹל זְרוֹעֲךָ יִדְּמוּ כָּאָבֶן. וְתִתֵּן בְּלֵב הַשָּׂרִים לְהֵיטִיב אֵלֵינוּ וּלְרַחֵם עָלֵינוּ. אוֹיְבֵינוּ יִלְבְּשׁוּ

פִּתְחוּ לִי פֶּתַח כְּחוּדוֹ שֶׁל מַחַט, וַאֲנִי אֶפְתַּח לָכֶם פֶּתַח כְּפִתְחוֹ שֶׁל אוּלָם — *Open for Me an entrance as tiny as a needlepoint and I, in turn, shall open for you an entrance as wide as the entrance of a hall.*

The source of this exact quotation is unknown. A similar version in *Shir HaShirim Rabbah* 5:3, reads: פִּתְחוּ לִי פֶּתַח אֶחָד שֶׁל תְּשׁוּבָה כְּחוּדָה שֶׁל מַחַט וַאֲנִי פּוֹתֵחַ לָכֶם פְּתָחִים שֶׁיִּהְיוּ עֲגָלוֹת וּקְרוֹנוֹת נִכְנָסוֹת, *Make Me a single opening of repentance like the point of a needle. Then I will provide you with entrances that wagons and carriages can enter.*

The *Mishnah (Middos 3:7)* states that the width of the entranceway of the אוּלָם, *hall*, was twenty cubits and its height was forty cubits. The *Gerrer Rebbe* noted that this entranceway was unique not only because of its size but also because it had no doors [see *Eruvin* 3b]. Thus, God promised Israel that if they would repent even slightly, He would keep the entrance of repentance [*teshuvah*] open for them at all times.

R' Yisroel Salanter compares repentance to needlepoint. He notes that although the hole made in needlepoint is tiny, it is penetrating, for it pierces the fabric completely and draws a thread behind it. Similarly, God welcomes repentance, even if the penitent rectifies only one tiny sin, if his repentance for

that transgression is complete and sincere. *R' Salanter* explains that if true contrition penetrates the depth of a man's heart, then it will draw in its wake much more genuine penitence.

וּרְאֵה כִּי אָזְלַת יָד וְאֶפֶס עָצוּר וְעָזוּב — *See! Their power is gone and there is no leader or helper* [Deuteronomy 32:36].

Earlier, Scripture says that God will judge Israel harshly for their sins. He will, however, take pity on them when He sees that they are utterly helpless and leaderless. If they turn to Him at that time — even if they are motivated primarily by desperation — God will accept their repentance.

וְחַנֹּתִי אֶת אֲשֶׁר אָחֹן וְרִחַמְתִּי אֶת אֲשֶׁר אֲרַחֵם — *I will be compassionate to those upon whom I favor, and I will be merciful to those whom I take mercy* (Exodus 33:19).

Maharil Diskin (comm. to *Parshas Vayishlach*) explains that God's blessing can sometimes become a curse. God knows that if some people are granted prosperity, they will become arrogant and defy God, or they will use their wealth to destroy their rivals and opponents. God knows that if He is compassionate to such people, He will eventually have to withdraw His compassion and unleash His wrath. Therefore, God is compassionate only to those who will

aglow as You promised us in Your great mercy: 'Open for Me an entrance as tiny as a needle point and I, in turn, will open for You an entrance as wide as the entrance of the Temple.'

See! Their power is gone and there is no leader or helper [Deut. 32:36]. *No one shows compassion or mercy except for You, for those whom You show compassion have experienced true compassion, and those whom You have shown mercy have experienced true mercy, as it is written:* I will be compassionate to those whom I favor and I will be merciful to those upon whom I take mercy [Exod. 33:19]. *Therefore, A pure heart create for us, O God, and a steadfast spirit renew within us.*

As for the fiery impulses of our hearts, may they be aroused in increasing constancy by Your love and Your Torah. Assist us, O God of our salvation, for the sake of Your Name's glory [Psalms 79:9].

May the New Year commence with its blessings, and save us from captivity, from exploitation, from the grip of every enemy, ambush, pirate or plunderer. Nullify their plans and foil their schemes. Fear and dread shall fall upon them, by the greatness of Your Arm they shall be stilled as stone [Exodus 15:16]. Incline the rulers to be kind to us and to show us compassion. Let our foes be clothed in shame [see Psalms 35:26, 132:18],

---

benefit and improve from His bounty and to whom He can continue to show compassion and mercy.

[This explains the preceding words of supplication: כִּי חֲנוּנֶיךָ הֵם חֲנוּנִים, *Because those to whom You show compassion experience true and enduring compassion.*]

לֵב טָהוֹר בְּרָא לָנוּ אֱלֹהֵינוּ — *A pure heart create for us, our God.*

This is based on *Psalms* 51:12: *A pure heart create for me, O God, and a steadfast spirit renew within me.*

David composed this psalm when Nathan the prophet came to chastise him for his relationship with Bath Sheba (see *Psalms* 51:2). David humbly accepted the rebuke and dedicated his entire being to wholehearted repentance.

וְרוּחַ נָכוֹן חַדֵּשׁ בְּקִרְבֵּנוּ — *And a steadfast spirit renew within us.*

Sforno renders נָכוֹן as synonymous with מוּכָן, *prepared.* David pleaded,

'Grant me an intellectual spirit capable of understanding God's ways and equipped to communicate these insights to others.'

תָּחֵל שָׁנָה וּבִרְכוֹתֶיהָ — *May the New Year commence with its blessings.*

This alludes to *Megillah* 31b, which teaches that the annual cycle of Sabbath Torah reading is designed so that all the curses enumerated in *Deuteronomy* will be read before *Rosh HaShanah.*

וְתִתֵּן בְּלֵב הַשָּׂרִים לְהֵיטִיב אֵלֵינוּ — *Incline the rulers to be kind to us.*

As Solomon said (*Proverbs* 21:1): פַּלְגֵי מַיִם לֶב מֶלֶךְ בְּיַד ה' עַל כָּל אֲשֶׁר יַחְפֹּץ יַטֶּנּוּ, *Like channels of water is the heart of the king in the hand of HASHEM, He inclines it in any direction He desires.*

אוֹיְבֵינוּ יִלְבְּשׁוּ בוֹשֶׁת — *Let our foes be clothed in shame.*

When they depart from this world, the wicked are clothed in garments

בְּוֹשֶׁת, וְעָלֵינוּ תְּרַחֵם בְּרוֹב רַחֲמֶיךָ, וְתֹאמַר דַּי לְצָרוֹתֵינוּ.

וְכָל הַרְפַּתְקֵי דְעָדוּ עָלֵינוּ יִהְיוּ לְכַפֵּר חַטֹּאתֵינוּ עֲוֹנוֹתֵינוּ וּפְשָׁעֵינוּ וְתֹאמַר דַּי לְצָרוֹתֵינוּ.

וּכְשֵׁם שֶׁחָשַׁבְתָּ עַל אֲבוֹתֵינוּ בַּמִּדְבָּר וְהִצַּלְתָּם מֵעֵינָא בִּישָׁא דְבִלְעָם כֵּן בְּצֵל כְּנָפֶיךָ תַּסְתִּירֵנוּ וְנִהְיֶה מְכוּסִים בְּמִכְסֵה וְהַנְהָגַת שְׁמוֹתֶיךָ הַקְּדוֹשִׁים, וְתִשְׁמְרֵם מִכָּל הֶפְסֵד וְכָל עֲלִילָה.

אָנָּא יהוה הוֹשִׁיעֵנוּ בִּזְכוּת אַבְרָהָם אִישׁ הַחֶסֶד, יִצְחָק אָזוּר בִּגְבוּרָה, יַעֲקֹב כְּלִיל תִּפְאֶרֶת, מֹשֶׁה רַעְיָא מְהֵימְנָא אָחוּז בְּנֶצַח, אַהֲרֹן אָחוּז בְּהוֹד, יוֹסֵף אָחוּז בִּיסוֹד, דָּוִד אָחוּז בְּמַלְכוּת, וּבִזְכוּתָם תַּצִּילֵנוּ מִיַּד אוֹיְבֵינוּ, וְתַהֲפוֹךְ לָבָם מֵרָעָה לְטוֹבָה. וְיִהְיֶה לָנוּ יְשׁוּב וְהַשְׁקֵט וָבֶטַח לַעֲבָדְךָ בֶּאֱמֶת, בְּלִי שׁוּם טִרְדָה.

fashioned from their own evil actions. They are covered with spiritual refuse and putrefaction, which disgraces them (R' Yeibi).

וְכָל הַרְפַּתְקֵי דְעָדוּ עָלֵינוּ יִהְיוּ לְכַפֵּר — *May all the calamities which befall us serve to atone.*

This is based on *Kiddushin* 33a; there the *Talmud* relates that R' Yochanan would arise in reverence not only for an elderly Jew, but even for old gentiles; he explained: כַּמָּה הַרְפַּתְקֵי עָדוּ עָלַיְיהוּ, *How many difficult experiences and calamities befell them* in the course of their long lives! Certainly they witnessed many miracles of Divine assistance.

Rashi explains that since these gentiles had witnessed Divine miracles, R' Yochanan deemed them worthy of reverence and respect. [Clearly, therefore, R' Yochanan teaches that every person can perceive the hand of God in his life, if he is but willing to do so.]

וְהִצַּלְתָּם מֵעֵינָא בִּישָׁא דְבִלְעָם — *And rescued them from Balaam's evil eye.*

Balaam would draw the forces of evil to any place where he would concentrate his jealous, vicious vision (*Zohar*).

The *Mishnah* (*Avos* 5:22) teaches that we still need protection against Balaam's threat: Whoever has within him these three faults is of the disciples of Balaam, the wicked — an evil eye, a haughty temperament, and an insatiable spirit.

בִּזְכוּת אַבְרָהָם אִישׁ הַחֶסֶד — *In the merit of Abraham, the man of Kindness.*

The attribute of חֶסֶד, *kindness*, was embodied by the Patriarch Abraham, who devoted his life to serving his fellow man [see *Micah* 7:20].

יִצְחָק אָזוּר בִּגְבוּרָה — *Isaac, who was girded with Might.*

The Patriarch Isaac represents גְּבוּרָה, *strength*, an uncompromising quest for perfection, and a fear of transgression that causes refrain from any act that falls short of the highest standard.

The *Talmud* relates that during the strict judgment of the End of Days, Isaac will be the meritorious one who will gain God's compassion for Israel.

יַעֲקֹב כְּלִיל תִּפְאֶרֶת — *Jacob, the perfection of Splendor.*

Jacob represents תִּפְאֶרֶת, *splendor*. This attribute combines חֶסֶד, *kindness*, and גְּבוּרָה, *might*, into the perfect blend.

Splendor is uniquely associated with Jacob because he was the paragon of אֱמֶת, *truth* [see *Micah* 7:20]. Truth results when all forces and attributes are properly balanced and harmonized in *splendor*.

מֹשֶׁה רַעְיָא מְהֵימְנָא — *Moses, the faithful*

while in Your abundant mercy show us compassion, and say 'enough' of our misfortunes.

May all the calamities which befall us serve to atone for our sins, iniquities and transgressions and may You say 'enough' of our misfortunes.

Just as You sheltered our fathers in the wilderness and rescued them from Balaam's evil eye, so too hide us in the shadow of Your wings [Psalms 17:8] so that we may be protected by a cloak and by the guidance of Your Holy Names. And may You safeguard them from every loss and every libel.

Please HASHEM, save us in the merit of Abraham, the man of Kindness; Isaac, who was girded with Might; Jacob, the perfection of Splendor; Moses, the faithful shepherd embraced by Eternity; Aaron, embraced by Majesty; Joseph, embraced by Foundation; and David, embraced by Kingship. In their merit save us from the hand of our enemies and transform their hearts from evil to good. May we have composure, quiet, and security so that we may serve You sincerely with no disturbance.

---

shepherd.

The *Zohar* gave this title for the greatest of all Jewish leaders, Moses, who selflessly led and tended his flock through the forty years in the wilderness.

מֹשֶׁה...אָחוּז בְּנֶצַח — *Moses...embraced by Eternity.*

The word נֶצַח can indicate *eternity* and *triumph*. These two concepts are related in that the one who triumphs over adversity can endure forever. Moses, the strong leader who overcame all obstacles and rebellions, personifies נֶצַח.

אַהֲרֹן אָחוּז בְּהוֹד — *Aaron, embraced by Majesty.*

This *Sefirah*, the eighth, complements the conquering aspect of נֶצַח, *eternity* and *triumph*, just as חֶסֶד, *kindness*, is the counterpoint of גְבוּרָה, *might*.

הוֹד, *majesty*, represents submission to circumstances, rather than an attempt to conquer them.

Moses did not hesitate to chastise the people when they rebelled against God. Aaron, however, was renowned for his compassion. He taught the people that

their *majesty* lay in accepting the circumstances which God had ordained for them.

יוֹסֵף אָחוּז בִּיסוֹד — *Joseph, embraced by Foundation.*

Joseph is commonly accorded the title יוֹסֵף הַצַּדִּיק, *Joseph the righteous*, because he overcame temptation and did not sin with Potiphar's wife.

In *Proverbs* (10:25), Solomon said, וְצַדִּיק יְסוֹד עוֹלָם, *the righteous man is the foundation of the world.*

יְסוֹד, *foundation*, is the ninth *sefirah*. The *sefiros* are arranged in descending order; the emanations proceed from the realm of abstract potential to the realm of fruition and actualization in This World. *Foundation* also serves the harmonizing function of bringing together all the preceding emanations and enabling them to enter the physical world. Therefore, יְסוֹד, *foundation*, is likened to the reproductive function of man, which brings life into the world. Since Joseph guarded this function and did not abuse it, he represents יְסוֹד.

דָוִד אָחוּז בְּמַלְכוּת — *David, embraced by Kingship.*

Kingship [מַלְכוּת] represents revela-

וְתִזַכֵּנוּ לְהִתְרַחֵק מֵהַגַּאֲוָה וְהַכַּעַס וְהַקְּפָּדָה וְכָל גּוֹבַהּ לֵב. וְנִהְיֶה מִיּוֹשְׁבִים בְּדַעְתֵּנוּ וְנַכִּיר מִיעוּט עֶרְכֵּנוּ. וְנַפְשֵׁנוּ כֶּעָפָר לַכֹּל תִּהְיֶה וְלֹא נִתְכַּעֵס וְלֹא נַקְפִּיד, וְנִהְיֶה אֹהֲבֵי שָׁלוֹם וּמַרְבִּים שָׁלוֹם.

וְתִזַכֵּנוּ לְהִתְרַחֵק מִלֵּצָנוּת, וְשֶׁקֶר וַחֲנוּפָה, וְלָשׁוֹן הָרָע, וְדִבּוּר שֶׁל חוֹל בְּשַׁבָּת, וְכָל דִּבּוּר אָסוּר. וְיִהְיֶה רוֹב דִּבּוּרֵנוּ בַּתּוֹרָה וּבְעִנְיְנֵי עֲבוֹדָתֶךָ. וּתְאַזְּרֵנוּ חַיִל לִשְׁמוֹר לְפִינוּ מַחְסוֹם מֵחֲטֹא בִלְשׁוֹנֵנוּ.

אָב הָרַחֲמָן, תֶּן בָּנוּ כֹּחַ וּבְרִיאוּת, וְזַכֵּנוּ לְהִתְרַחֵק מִתַּאֲוַת תַּעֲנוּגֵי וְהֶבְלֵי הָעוֹלָם הַזֶּה, וְנֹאכַל לְשׂוֹבַע נַפְשֵׁנוּ, וְכֵן בְּכָל צָרְכֵנוּ יִהְיוּ כָל מַעֲשֵׂינוּ לְשֵׁם שָׁמַיִם.

וּתְזַכֵּנוּ לִהְיוֹת שְׂמֵחִים בְּעֵסֶק תּוֹרָתֶיךָ וּמִצְוֹתֶיךָ וְלִהְיוֹת בְּטוּחוֹנֵנוּ בְּךָ תָּדִיר, וְיִהְיֶה לָנוּ לֵב שָׂמֵחַ לַעֲבוֹדָתֶךָ.

אָנָּא, מֶלֶךְ רַחוּם וְחַנּוּן, הַנְּשָׁמָה לָךְ וְהַגּוּף פְּעָלֶךָ, חוּסָה עַל עֲמָלֶךָ. וּבְכֵן יֶהֱמוּ רַחֲמֶיךָ עָלֵינוּ, וּתְזַכֵּנוּ לְהַשְׁלִים תִּקּוּן נַפְשׁוֹתֵנוּ רוּחוֹתֵנוּ נִשְׁמוֹתֵנוּ וְלֹא נֹאבַד, חַס וְשָׁלוֹם.

וְתִזַכֵּנוּ לַעֲסוֹק בְּתוֹרָתֶךָ הַקְּדוֹשָׁה וּלְכַוֵּין לַאֲמִתָּהּ שֶׁל תּוֹרָה. וְתַצִּילֵנוּ מִכָּל טָעוּת בַּהֲלָכָה וּבְהוֹרָאָה וְאַל תַּצֵל מִפִּינוּ דְּבַר אֱמֶת לְעוֹלָם.

וְנִהְיֶה אֲנַחְנוּ, וְצֶאֱצָאֵינוּ, וְצֶאֱצָאֵי צֶאֱצָאֵינוּ, כֻּלָּנוּ יוֹדְעֵי שְׁמֶךָ, וְלוֹמְדֵי תוֹרָתֶךָ לִשְׁמָהּ, וּמְקַיְּמֵי מִצְוֹתֶיךָ. וְלֹא יִמָּצֵא בָנוּ, וְלֹא בְזַרְעֵנוּ וְזֶרַע זַרְעֵנוּ, שׁוּם פְּגָם וְשׁוּם פָּסוּל. וְלֹא יִתְחַלֵּל שִׁמְךָ עַל יָדֵינוּ, חַס וְשָׁלוֹם.

וּרְאֵה כִּי עַמְּךָ הַגּוֹי הַגָּדוֹל הַזֶּה, זֶרַע אֲהוּבֶיךָ, אַבְרָהָם, יִצְחָק, וְיִשְׂרָאֵל עֲבָדֶיךָ, בָּנֶיךָ בְּנֵי בְחוּנֶיךָ, וְזֶה כַּמָּה מֵאוֹת

---

tion of God's will in the material world and the recognition of His sovereignty.

David, the sweet singer of Israel, established the royal line of Jewish kings. He personifies this emanation, because the majesty of the true Jewish king is a reflection of God's sovereignty on earth.

וְנַפְשֵׁנוּ כֶּעָפָר לַכֹּל תִּהְיֶה — *Let our spirits be like dust to everyone.*

This is based on the words which Mar bar Ravina would say after concluding the *Amidah* service (see *Berachos* 17a).

The commentators explain that al-

though people constantly trample the dust and the soil, this dirt never refuses to give forth its produce to man. We pray that even when people offend and insult us, we will act generously towards them.

וְנִהְיֶה אֲנַחְנוּ, וְצֶאֱצָאֵינוּ... — *Let us and our offspring...*

The ensuing lines are part of the text of the בִּרְכַּת הַתּוֹרָה, *the benediction over Torah study*, as recorded in the *Talmud* (*Berachos* 11b).

נָא גִבּוֹר, דּוֹרְשֵׁי יִחוּדְךָ כְּבָבַת שָׁמְרֵם — *Please, Powerful One, guard those who*

Grant us the privilege of being divorced from arrogance, anger, irritability, and every kind of conceit.

May our minds be at ease. May we recognize our insignificance. Let our spirits be like dust to everyone. Let us not be angered or irritated, and may we be lovers of peace and promoters of peace.

Grant us the privilege of being divorced from scorn, falsehood, flattery, tale-bearing, mundane conversation on the Sabbath, and any form of forbidden speech. May most of our conversations be inTorah and in matters concerning Your service. Gird us with the strength to guard our mouths with a muzzle lest we sin with our tongue.

Father of Mercy! Give us strength and health. Grant us the privilege of being divorced from lust and the vain pleasures of This World. May we eat only to satisfy our souls, so, too, regarding all of our needs, may all our actions be for the sake of Heaven.

Grant us the privilege of being joyful with regard to Your Torah and Your commandments. May our trust be placed in You always and may we have a heart gladdened by Your service.

Please, O King, Merciful and Compassionate, the spirit is Yours, and the body is Your work, have pity on Your labor. Therefore, let Your Mercy yearn for us, and grant us the privilege of completing the perfection of our lives, spirits, and souls, so that we may not be doomed, Heaven forbid.

Grant us the privilege of engaging in the study of Your holy Torah and allow us to comprehend the true meaning of the Torah. Rescue us from any error, in halachic decision or instruction, and do not remove the word of truth from our mouth, forever [Psalms 119:43].

Let us and our offspring and the offspring of our offspring — all of us — be among those who know Your Name, who study Your Torah for its own sake, and who fulfill Your commandments. Let there not be found in us, or in our children, or in our children's children, any defect or disqualification. May Your Name not be desecrated by us, Heaven forbid.

Observe that Your people, this great nation — the children of Your beloved ones, Abraham, Isaac, and Israel, Your servants; Your children, children of Your tested ones — have by now en-

---

seek Your Oneness, like the apple of Your eye.

This is the third line of the Kab-

balistic poem אָנָא בְּכֹחַ which is attributed to the holy Tanna, R' Nechunya ben HaKaneh. It is based on

שָׁנִים בְּלָחֲצָם וְדוֹחֲקָם, קוֹרְאִים בְּשִׁמְךָ, וּמַאֲמִינִים בְּךָ וּבְתוֹרָתֶךָ. וְכַמָּה אֲלָפִים וּרְבָבוֹת מָסְרוּ עַצְמָן עַל קְדוּשָׁתֶךָ. וְהֵם מְלֵאִים מִצְוֹת וְצִדְקוֹת וְתוֹרָה וּגְמִילוּת חֲסָדִים. נָא גִבּוֹר, דּוֹרְשֵׁי יִחוּדְךָ כְּבָבַת שָׁמְרֵם:

אָנָּא, מֶלֶךְ רַחוּם וְחַנּוּן, הִתְמַלֵּא רַחֲמִים עַל כָּל אַחֵינוּ בְּנֵי יִשְׂרָאֵל הַנְּפוֹצִים בְּאַרְבַּע כַּנְפוֹת הָאָרֶץ, וּבִפְרָט עַל יוֹשְׁבֵי אֶרֶץ יִשְׂרָאֵל, וְעַל יוֹשְׁבֵי הָעִיר הַזּוֹ, וְעַל כָּל הַקְּהָל הַקָּדוֹשׁ הַזֶּה, וּתְרַחֵם עָלֵינוּ וַעֲלֵיהֶם, וְתַצִּילֵנוּ וְתַצִּילֵם מֵרָעָה, מֵרָעָב, וּמִשֶּׁבִי, וּמִבִּזָּה, וּמִכָּל חֵטְא.

וְתִשְׁלַח רְפוּאָה שְׁלֵמָה לְכָל חוֹלֵי עַמְּךָ יִשְׂרָאֵל, אֵל נָא רְפָא נָא לָהֶם. וּתְקַיֵּם בְּכָל אֶחָד מֵהֶם מִקְרָא שֶׁכָּתוּב, יְהוה יִסְעָדֶנּוּ עַל עֶרֶשׂ דְּוָי, כָּל מִשְׁכָּבוֹ הָפַכְתָּ בְחָלְיוֹ. וְהַבְּרִיאִים מֵדוֹרְשֶׁיךָ, תַּתְמִיד בְּרִיאוּתָם שֶׁלֹּא יֶחֱלוּ, חַס וְשָׁלוֹם, וְתַצִּילֵנוּ וְתַצִּיל לְכָל יִשְׂרָאֵל מִכָּל נֶזֶק, וּמִכָּל צַר, וּמַשְׁטִין, וּמְקַטְרֵג, וּמֵרוּחַ רָעָה,

God's secret, Holy Name of forty-two letters (*Kiddushin* 71a). This name is revealed only to people of rare holiness (*Tikkun Tefillah*).

All Jews seek the revelation of the Oneness of God's Name, for the Jewish nation is dedicated to teaching the world that God controls every phase of creation.

אָנָּא מֶלֶךְ — Please, O King.

The *Talmud* (*Berachos* 54b) teaches that there are four cases in which people are obligated to offer thanks to God for their salvation: 1) when a person returns safely from a sea voyage; 2) when someone crosses the desert unharmed; 3) when a person recovers from a serious illness and 4) when a person is released from prison. This supplication begs God to rescue the people whose lives are endangered by such perils. This prayer is most appropriate for *Rosh Hashanah*, when all lives hang in the balance and are judged by the Heavenly Tribunal.

וְתִשְׁלַח רְפוּאָה שְׁלֵמָה לְכָל חוֹלֵי עַמְּךָ יִשְׂרָאֵל — *Send u complete recovery to all the sick of Your people, Israel.*

Even when a doctor seems to have cured his patient, he can never guarantee that the malady will not return. However, when God heals the sick, the cure is permanent.

אֵל נָא רְפָא נָא לָהֶם — *O God, please! Heal them, now!*

This based on *Numbers* 12:13. When Miriam spoke disparagingly of her brother, Moses, she was afflicted with leprosy. Moses forgave her and prayed on her behalf, רְפָא נָא לָהּ, *heal her now!*

ה' יִסְעָדֶנּוּ עַל עֶרֶשׂ דְּוָי — *HASHEM will fortify him on his bed of misery.*

The *Talmud* (*Shabbos* 12b) derives from this verse that God supplies the invalid with strength and nutrition, and that the שְׁכִינָה, *Divine Presence*, rests at the head of every sick bed. Therefore, a visitor should not sit on an invalid's bed [for this would imply irreverence for the *Shechinah*].

כָּל מִשְׁכָּבוֹ הָפַכְתָּ בְחָלְיוֹ — *All his restfulness [lit. bedding] has been upset by his illness.*

This translations follows *Rashi* and *Radak*, who interpret חָלְיוֹ as the most severe stage of *his illness* and מִשְׁכָּבוֹ as *his restfulness.*

Radak offers another interpretation:

dured numerous centuries of oppression and hardship. Still they call upon Your Name, and believe in You and Your Torah. Many thousands and myriads have martyred themselves to sanctify Your Name. They are filled with good deeds, acts of charity, Torah knowledge, and acts of kindness. Please, Powerful One, guard those who seek Your Oneness, like the apple of Your eye.

Please, O King, Merciful and Compassionate, be full of mercy on all our brethren, the Children of Israel, who are scattered through the four corners of the earth; and particularly the inhabitants of Eretz Yisrael, on the inhabitants of this city, and on this entire holy congregation. Have mercy on us and on them. Rescue us and rescue them from evil, famine, captivity, plunder, and from all sins.

Send complete recovery to all the sick of Your people, Israel. O God, please! Heal them, now! [Numbers 12:13]. Fulfill for each of them the Scriptural verse: HASHEM will fortify him on his bed of misery, all his restfulness has been upset by his illness [Psalms 41:4]. As for the healthy ones who seek You — sustain their health, that they may not be ill, Heaven forbid. Rescue us and rescue all of Israel from any injury, from any tormentor, persecutor, accuser, from spirit of depression, from the sharp

Despite the severity of the illness, You provided the invalid with the strength to turn from side to side on his bed.

וְהַבְּרִיאִים מְדוֹרְשֶׁיךָ, תַּתְמִיד בְּרִיאוּתָם — As for the healthy ones who seek You—sustain their health.

The Sages emphasize that even a slight ailment should not be taken lightly, because it is a sign of God's displeasure. If the warning is ignored, more serious maladies may follow.

A person should always implore Divine mercy that he not fall ill, because once he does become ill they [the heavenly forces] tell him, 'Bring proof of your virtues and merits; only then will you be released!' If one senses even a slight headache he should feel like a prisoner placed in chains. If his health deteriorates to the point where he is confined to bed, he should consider himself like a person on trial for his life

who can be saved only by the most powerful and influential defenders (Shabbos 32a).

וְתַצִּילֵנוּ ... מִכָּל צַר וּמַשְׂטִין, וּמְקַטְרֵג — And save us from any tormentor, persecutor, accuser.

The Talmud (Bava Basra 16b) teaches that all the diverse aspects of evil are really a single force cloaked in different guises. First, the יֵצֶר הָרַע, Evil Inclination, descends to earth to seduce a man to sin. Then the Evil One rises heavenward and appears before the Heavenly Tribunal as שָׂטָן הַמְקַטְרֵג, the accusing prosecutor, demanding punishment for the offender. Once a guilty verdict is issued, the Evil One is sent to earth as the מַלְאַךְ הַמָּוֶת, the Angel of Death, to carry out the Heavenly sentence.

The Rabbis taught that Satan exerts greater effort to accuse and harm a

וּמִדְקְדוּקֵי עֲנִיּוּת, וּמִכָּל מִינֵי פּוּרְעָנִיּוֹת הַמִּתְרַגְּשׁוֹת בָּעוֹלָם.

וְתִפְקוֹד בְּזֶרַע שֶׁל קַיָּמָא, זֶרַע קוֹדֶשׁ, לְכָל חֲשׂוּכֵי בָנִים.

וְהַיּוֹשְׁבוֹת עַל הַמַּשְׁבֵּר, תּוֹצִיאֵם מֵאֲפֵלָה לְאוֹרָה, וְיֵצֵא הַוָּלָד

בְּשָׁעָה טוֹבָה, וְלֹא יְאֻרַע שׁוּם צַעַר וָנֶזֶק, לֹא לַיּוֹלְדוֹת וְלֹא

לְיַלְדֵיהֶן, וְאַל יִמְשׁוֹל אַסְכְּרָה וְשֵׁדִין בְּכָל יַלְדֵי עַמְּךָ יִשְׂרָאֵל,

וּתְגַדְּלֵם לְתוֹרָתֶךָ וּמִצְוֹתֶיךָ בְּחַיֵּי אֲבִיהֶם וְאִמָּם. וּבְנֵי יִשְׂרָאֵל

עַמְּךָ יוֹרְדֵי הַיָּם בָּאֳנִיּוֹת, פְּצֵם וְהַצִּילֵם מִמַּיִם רַבִּים, מִיַּד בְּנֵי

נֵכָר. הַצִּילֵם מִטִּיט וְאַל יִטְבָּעוּ יִנָּצְלוּ מִשְּׂנֵאִים וּמִשַּׂנְאִים

וּמִמַּעֲמַקֵּי מָיִם.

וּבְנֵי יִשְׂרָאֵל הַהוֹלְכִים בַּיַּבָּשָׁה, הַדְרִיכֵם בְּדֶרֶךְ יְשָׁרָה,

לָלֶכֶת אֶל עִיר מוֹשָׁב, וְהַצִּילֵם מִכַּף כָּל אוֹיֵב וְאוֹרֵב בַּדָּרֶךְ.

וְכָל הָאֲסוּרִים בַּכֶּלֶא בְּלֹא מִשְׁפָּט מֵעַמְּךָ יִשְׂרָאֵל, הַתֵּר

מֵאֲסָרֵיהֶם, וְתוֹצִיאֵם לִרְוָחָה, וּתְשִׂימֵם לְיִרְאָתֶךָ.

וְתָחוֹן זְכוּת אָבוֹת לְהוֹצִיא לָאוֹר מִשְׁפָּטֵנוּ, כָּתְבֵנוּ בְּסֵפֶר

חַיִּים, לְמַעַנְךָ אֱלֹהִים חַיִּים, וְהָאֵר פָּנֶיךָ עַל מִקְדָּשְׁךָ הַשָּׁמֵם,

לְמַעַן אֲדֹנָי. יָשָׁר, פּוֹדֶה, חוּס וְרַחֵם עָלֵינוּ, וּשְׁמַע תְּפִלָּתֵנוּ, כִּי

רַחוּם אָתָּה.

אֱלֹהֵינוּ וֵאלֹהֵי אֲבוֹתֵינוּ, מֶלֶךְ רַחֲמָן רַחֵם עָלֵינוּ,
טוֹב וּמֵטִיב הִדָּרֶשׁ לָנוּ. שׁוּבָה אֵלֵינוּ

---

person who is in danger (*Rashi, Genesis* 42:4; *Deut*. 23:10).

However, at the very time of Satan's accusation, the angel Michael defends Israel and enumerates her many virtues and merits (*Shemos Rabbah* 18:5).

וּמֵרוּחַ רָעָה, וּמִדְקְדּוּקֵי עֲנִיּוּת — *From spirit of depression and from sharp pangs of poverty.*

The Rabbis taught that three things can pervert a man's mind and drive him away from God: Idol worship, a melancholy spirit, and the pangs of dire poverty (*Eruvin* 41b).

וְהַיּוֹשְׁבוֹת עַל הַמַּשְׁבֵּר, תּוֹצִיאֵם מֵאֲפֵלָה לְאוֹרָה...וְלֹא יְאֻרַע שׁוּם צַעַר וָנֶזֶק, לֹא לְיוֹלְדוֹת וְלֹא לְיַלְדֵיהֶן — *And as for mothers in labor, withdraw them from darkness to light...may no pain of harm befall either mothers or their newborn infants.*

The *Mishnah* (*Shabbos* 2:6) teaches that women sometimes die in childbirth

as punishment for their sins. The *Talmud* (*Shabbos* 32a) notes that when a woman is physically healthy, even relatively minor merits can protect her; at childbirth, however, the danger is so great that only a miracle can save her life. At that time, her sins may render her unworthy of Divine assistance (see *Rashi, Shabbos* 32a s.v. אַבָּב חוּטְרָא מִילֵי).

וְאַל יִמְשׁוֹל אַסְכְּרָה וְשֵׁדִין — *May neither croup nor evil forces hold sway among the infants.*

According to the *Talmud* (*Berachos* 8a), there are nine hundred and three ways of dying. The most difficult of all is croup which is likened to a sharp thorn stuck in a ball of wool. The wool becomes entangled with the thorn; any attempt to free the thorn tears the wool.

The *Talmud* (*Shabbos* 33a) says that an attack of croup is punishment for לְשׁוֹן הָרַע, *slander*. [Since a person who

pangs of poverty, and from any forms of retribution which agitate against the world.

Remember with surviving offspring — holy offspring — all who are deprived of children. And as for mothers in labor, withdraw them from darkness to light. May the infant emerge at a propitious time, and may no pain or harm befall either mothers or their newborn infants. May neither croup nor evil forces hold sway among the infants of Your people, Israel. Let them grow to Your Torah and commandments in the lifetimes of their father and mother.

As for the sons of Your people, Israel, who go down to the sea in ships [Psalms 107:23], free them and rescue them from the watery expanse, from alien power. Rescue them from the mire so that they sink not [Psalms 69:15]. Let them be saved from enemies and from turbulent waters [Psalms 43; see Psalms 65:8 and 74:23] and from the watery depth.

And as for the Children of Israel who travel over land, lead them on a straight route to arrive at an inhabited city. Save them from the grips of every enemy or ambusher along the way.

And as for all those unjustly imprisoned in dungeons from among Your nation, Israel, release their shackles, liberate them to expansive freedom, and establish them to fear You.

Grant us graciously the merit of our forefathers to bring our verdict to light. Inscribe us in the Book of Life, for Your sake, O living God. Let Your face glow upon Your desolate Temple, for the sake of my Lord. O Upright One, Redeemer — take pity and have mercy on us. Hear our prayers, for You are merciful.

Our God and the God of our fathers, O Merciful King, have mercy on us. Good and Beneficent One, be responsive to us. Return to us with Your abundant mercy

slanders others misuses his throat and vocal chords, he is afflicted with croup which affects precisely those parts of the body that were involved in his sin.]

הַהוֹלְכִים בַּיַּבָּשָׁה, הַדְרִיכֵם בְּדֶרֶךְ יְשָׁרָה — Who travel over land, lead them on a straight route.

The traveler requires Divine assistance to negotiate these difficult passages and obstacles.

As *Sifri* (*Deut.* 20) states: There is no road which does not have crooked parts; there is no road which does not have pitfalls; there is no road which does not have forks and crossroads.

אֱלֹהֵינוּ וֵאלֹהֵי אֲבוֹתֵינוּ — Our God and the God of our fathers.

מֶלֶךְ רַחֲמָן רַחֵם עָלֵינוּ — O Merciful King, have mercy upon us.

This section is taken from the *Musaf Shemoneh Esrei* service of שָׁלֹשׁ רְגָלִים, the three pilgrimage festivals. Since the service of the festivals formerly centered around the Temple, the loss of that holiest of structures is most keenly felt during our festival celebrations. This supplication gives voice to Israel's yearning to see the Temple rebuilt.

A great question arises as to whether God will rebuild the Temple with His

בַּהֲמוֹן רַחֲמֶיךָ, בִּגְלַל אָבוֹת שֶׁעָשׂוּ רְצוֹנֶךָ, בְּנֵה בֵיתְךָ
כְּבַתְּחִלָּה, וְכוֹנֵן מִקְדָּשְׁךָ עַל מְכוֹנוֹ, וְהַרְאֵנוּ בְּבִנְיָנוֹ,
וְשַׂמְּחֵנוּ בְּתִקּוּנוֹ, וְהָשֵׁב שְׁכִינָתְךָ לְתוֹכוֹ, וְהָשֵׁב
כֹּהֲנִים לַעֲבוֹדָתָם וּלְוִיִּם לְדוּכָנָם, וְהָשֵׁב יִשְׂרָאֵל
לִנְוֵיהֶם, וּמַלְּאָה הָאָרֶץ דֵּעָה, לְיִרְאָה אֶת שִׁמְךָ הַגָּדוֹל
הַגִּבּוֹר וְהַנּוֹרָא. אָמֵן כֵּן יְהִי רָצוֹן, אָמֵן וְאָמֵן.

מִדַּת הָרַחֲמִים, *Attribute of Mercy*, or with His מִדַּת הַדִּין, *Attribute of Strict Justice.*

טוֹב וּמֵטִיב — *Good and Beneficent One.*

This is based on *Psalms* 119:68, טוֹב, אַתָּה וּמֵטִיב, *good are You, and beneficent.* You are *Good* even when You are not asked for kindness, and *beneficent* to those who request it (*Metzudas David*).

Iyun Tefillah observes that some people are good-hearted by nature, but lack the means to be beneficent to others. Other people are hard-hearted by nature, yet they force themselves to be beneficent to others in order to fulfill the demands and precepts of the Torah.

But the Almighty is both innately *Good* and superbly endowed with the means to be *Beneficent* to all.

הִדָּרֶשׁ לָנוּ — *Be responsive to us.*

[This phrase is based on *Ezekiel* 36:37: כֹּה אָמַר אֲדֹנָי ה' עוֹד זֹאת אִדָּרֵשׁ לְבֵית יִשְׂרָאֵל לַעֲשׂוֹת לָהֶם אַרְבֶּה אֹתָם כַּצֹּאן אָדָם, *So says my Lord HASHEM: 'I will once again accede to the request of the house of Israel to work for them, I will multiply them, to make man as plentiful as sheep.'*

I will allow myself to be persuaded by their prayers, and I will give in to their pleas (*Rashi*).

שׁוּבָה אֵלֵינוּ — *Return to us.*

As the prophet says (*Malachi* 3:7):

שׁוּבוּ אֵלַי וְאָשׁוּבָה אֲלֵיכֶם, *Return to Me, and I will return to You.* The ה, *heh,* appended to שׁוּב, *return,* denotes intense desire (*Iyin Tefillah*). Also, it alludes to the verse (*Isaiah* 30:15): בְּשׁוּבָה וָנַחַת תִּוָּשֵׁעוּן, *with tranquility and ease you will be saved* (*Eitz Yoseif*).

בִּגְלַל אָבוֹת שֶׁעָשׂוּ רְצוֹנֶךָ — *For the sake of the Patriarchs who did Your will.*

Scripture assured the children of Israel, *For a God of mercy is HASHEM, Your God, He will not loosen His grip on you, neither will He destroy you, and He will not forget the covenant of your fathers, that which He promised to them* (*Deut.* 4:31).

In *Leviticus* (Ch. 26), Scripture provides a detailed description of the calamities and devastation which will befall the Jewish people if they abandon God and betray His covenant. Nevertheless, even after Israel's treachery, God reiterates His promise, *And I shall remember My covenant with Jacob, and even my covenant with Isaac, and even my covenant with Abraham I shall remember, and I shall remember the land* (*Lev.* 26:43).[1]

בְּנֵה בֵיתְךָ כְּבַתְּחִלָּה — *Rebuild Your House as in former times.*

The *Midrash* (*Bereishis Rabbah* 13:2) says that Israel's prayers still center on the reconstruction of the Temple: 'Master, rebuild the Temple! Master,

1. The commentators observe that God is obligated, as it were, to preserve the existence of Israel for two reasons: 1) זְכוּת אָבוֹת, *the merits of the Patriarchs,* who fulfilled His every demand and always adhered to His will. 2) בְּרִית אָבוֹת, *the covenant* God made with the Patriarchs.

Some commentators maintain that the merit of the Patriarchs endured only as long as their descendants followed their example and adhered to God's will. When Israel forsook God's ways, He abandoned them and 'forgot' the merits of their forbears. Thus, according to this

for the sake of the Patriarchs who did Your will. Rebuild Your house as in former times and establish Your Sanctuary on its foundation. Show us its rebuilding and gladden us in its perfection. Return Your Shechinah to its midst; return the kohanim to their service and the Levites to their platform; and return Israel back to its dwellings. And may the earth be filled with knowledge [Isaiah 11:9] to fear Your Name — the Great, the Mighty, and the Awesome. Amen. May such be Your will. Amen, amen.

---

rebuild the *Beis HaMikdash!*'

The *Yerushalmi* (*Yoma* 1:1) condemns Israel for failing in their prayers: Every generation for whom the *Beis HaMikdash* is not rebuilt is considered as if it caused its destruction.

The prayer is that God, *Himself,* rebuild it.

The first and second Temples were built by human hands; the third one, however, will be built by the hands of the Almighty Himself (*Rashi, Succah* 41a, *Rosh HaShanah* 30a; *Tosafos, Shavuos* 15b).

Rambam, however, appears to have a different opinion. He emphasizes that the king Messiah will be the one to rebuild the *Beis HaMikdash* and gather in the exiles of Israel (*Hilchos Melachim* 11:1,4).

Some commentators explain that if Israel's fervent prayers and fulfillment of the precepts merit that the date of redemption be hastened (אֲחִישֶׁנָה), then the Temple will descend from heaven immediately in fiery form. But if Israel fails to generate enthusiasm and fiery yearning for the Temple, then the redemption will have to wait for its preordained time (בְּעִתּוֹ). In the latter course of events, reconstruction will follow a natural course, through the hands of men, under the direction of the Messiah.

וְהַרְאֵנוּ בְּבִנְיָנוֹ, וְשַׂמְּחֵנוּ בְּתִקּוּנוֹ — *Show us its rebuilding, and gladden us in its perfection.*

Maharil Diskin interpreted this passage in light of the verse: טָבְעוּ בָאָרֶץ שְׁעָרֶיהָ, *Her gates sunk into the earth* (*Lamentations* 2:9). Although the *Beis HaMikdash* was destroyed, it is destined to be completely rebuilt; why, then, were its gates swallowed by the earth, rather than destroyed?

The third *Beis HaMikdash* will be rebuilt by God in fire. When the Jews behold this wondrous edifice, their joy will be tinged with sorrow and disappointment because they will be deprived of the opportunity to participate in the reconstruction.

Therefore, God preserved intact the original gates which had been built by Israel. He will permit the Jews to attach these gates to the fiery edifice. The *Talmud* (*Bava Basra* 52b) rules that the person who puts up protective gates on a house is considered as if he built the entire house. Thus, after the Jews *behold the rebuilding* by God of the Sanctuary, they will *rejoice in its completion,* when they put up its gates (*Siddur HaGRA; Siach Yitzchak*).

וּלְוִיִם לְדוּכָנָם — *And Levites to their platform.*

The Levites performed their chanting

---

view, only the eternal inviolable covenant of the Patriarchs survives to protect Israel [see *Shabbos* 55a and *Tosafos* s.v. שְׁמוּאֵל אָמַר תַּמָּה זְכוּת אָבוֹת].

Iyun Tefillah notes that this liturgical passage supports the view that the merit of the Patriarchs endures because we implore God to redeem us not merely because of the covenant but also *for the sake of the Patriarchs who did Your will.*

כָּל-כְּלִי יוּצַר עָלַיִךְ לֹא יִצְלָח, וְכָל לָשׁוֹן
תָּקוּם-אִתָּךְ לַמִּשְׁפָּט תַּרְשִׁיעִי, זֹאת
נַחֲלַת עַבְדֵי יהוה וְצִדְקָתָם מֵאִתִּי, נְאֻם יהוה:

לֹא-יָרֵעוּ וְלֹא-יַשְׁחִיתוּ בְּכָל-הַר קָדְשִׁי, כִּי-
מָלְאָה הָאָרֶץ דֵּעָה אֶת-יהוה, כַּמַּיִם לַיָּם
מְכַסִּים:

שִׁיר הַמַּעֲלוֹת, מִמַּעֲמַקִּים קְרָאתִיךָ יהוה: אֲדֹנָי
שִׁמְעָה בְקוֹלִי, תִּהְיֶינָה אָזְנֶיךָ
קַשֻּׁבוֹת, לְקוֹל תַּחֲנוּנָי: אִם עֲוֹנוֹת תִּשְׁמָר יָהּ אֲדֹנָי, מִי

on a דוכן, *platform* in the Temple court- yard.	The word נָוֶה is related to נָאֶה, *pleas- ant.* When Israel returns to the Holy Land, the Jews will find their *dwelling*
וְהָשֵׁב יִשְׂרָאֵל לִנְוֵיהֶם — *And return Israel back to its dwelling.*	*places* to be pleasant.

§§ שִׁיר הַמַּעֲלוֹת — A song of Ascents.

The New Year commences. The Jew has repented and shed his burden of bygone sins, but what has he done to rid himself of the factors that *caused* him to sin? Who can fathom the source of sin, the deep and complex emotions which lead man towards error and transgression? True inner purity cannot be attained without in- ner searching and cleansing.

Rambam places great emphasis on this point in the final words of *Hilchos Mikvaos* (11:12): The man who immerses himself in the waters of ritual purifica- tion rids himself of his contamination even though he has surely not made any significant physical changes in his body. Similarly, one who concentrates on cleans- ing himself of evil thoughts and sinful ideas, in effect immerses his soul in the waters of pure wisdom.

The *Midrash* (*Vayikra Rabbah* 3:7) stresses that only a deep and comprehensive knowledge of Torah can penetrate the depths of man, overcoming his dark passions and enlightening his troubled spirit. King Solomon said (*Proverbs* 20:5): מַיִם עֲמֻקִּים עֵצָה בְלֶב-אִישׁ וְאִישׁ תְּבוּנָה יִדְלֶנָּה, *Counsel in the heart of man is like deep water, but a man of understanding will draw it up.* Therefore, concludes the *Midrash,* when David composed *A Song of Ascents,* he began, *Out of the depths I called You, HASHEM;* he intended to ascend from the grip of sin, and his way of doing so was by climbing the rungs of Torah.

שִׁיר הַמַּעֲלוֹת — *A song of ascents.* Fifteen psalms (120-134) begin with these words (although Psalm 121 con- tains a minor difference). These fifteen songs of ascents correspond to the fif- teen steps leading up to the inner court- yard of the Temple. As the procession	ascended step by step into the holy area bringing water for the special service of *Succos,* groups of Levites stood on the steps singing the fifteen psalms in turn (*Succos* 51b). The commentators note that all fif- teen psalms refer to Jewish prayers that

'Any weapon sharpened against you shall not succeed, and any tongue that shall rise against you in judgment You shall condemn. This is the heritage of the servant of HASHEM, and their righteousness shall come from Me,' says HASHEM [Isaiah 54:17].

They shall neither injure nor destroy in all of My sacred mount, for the earth shall be filled with knowledge of HASHEM, as water covers the sea [Isaiah 11:9].

A song of Ascents. From the depth, I called You, HASHEM. O my Lord, hear my voice, let Your ears be attentive to the sound of my pleas. If you keep account of iniquities, YAH, my Lord, who could withstand? For

our people may *ascend* from exile and return to *Eretz Yisrael* and rebuild the Temple. *Hirsch* comments that this series of psalms constitutes a spiritual ladder of fifteen steps by means of which a Jew transcends the misery of oppressive circumstances [see ArtSroll *Bircas Hamazon*, 33].

מִמַּעֲמַקִּים קְרָאתִיךָ ה' — *From the depths I called You, HASHEM.*

This composition speaks for all men who are drowning in their respective depths of misfortune; however, the specific setting of the psalm is the tragic exile in which Israel is trapped *(Ibn Ezra; Radak; Meiri).*

Midrash Shocher Tov relates that Israel cried out to God, 'When will You redeem us?' The Almighty replied, 'When you sink to the lowest depths!' Therefore, the plural form מַעֲמַקִּים, *depths,* is employed to signify that Israel has descended from depth to depth until it can fall no further *(Mizmor L'Sodah).*

Nevertheless, despite its woes and harsh lot, Israel still perceives God as ה', *the Dispenser of Mercy,* and calls upon Him for compassion *(Alshich).*

אֲדֹנָי שִׁמְעָה בְקוֹלִי — *O my Lord, hear my voice.*

Because I am stranded in the depths

with no one else to help me, You alone must hear my voice and extricate me from these dire straits *(Radak).*

The *Talmud (Pesachim 50a)* teaches that the revelation of God's glory is severely diminished when Israel is in exile. God's Four-Letter Name is written in the Torah, but that Name may be pronounced as it is spelled only when the *Beis HaMikdash* stands. When Israel languishes in exile and the Divine splendor is eclipsed, God is merely called אֲדֹנָי, *my Lord.* Therefore, the exiles call out, שִׁמְעָה בְקוֹלִי, *hear my voice;* listen to my prayer even though in my exile, I cannot utter Your Name ה', *HASHEM,* but only Your secondary appellation אֲדֹנָי, *my Lord (R' Pinchas HaLevi Horowitz in Sefer HaMakneh).*

תִּהְיֶינָה אָזְנֶיךָ קַשֻּׁבוֹת, לְקוֹל תַּחֲנוּנָי — *Let Your ears be attentive to the sound of my pleas.*

Listen closely to the very *sound* — the tone of my voice, and You will detect that my words are the sincere expression of my innermost anguish and fear. Give ear to my tone of voice and You will be convinced that I place confidence in You alone' *(R' Yehuda Muskato).*

אִם עֲוֹנוֹת תִּשְׁמׇר יָהּ — *If You keep account of iniquities, YAH.*

יַעֲמֹד: כִּי עִמְּךָ הַסְּלִיחָה, לְמַעַן תִּוָּרֵא: קִוִּיתִי יהוה קִוְּתָה נַפְשִׁי, וְלִדְבָרוֹ הוֹחָלְתִּי: נַפְשִׁי לַאדֹנָי, מִשֹּׁמְרִים לַבֹּקֶר, שֹׁמְרִים לַבֹּקֶר: יַחֵל יִשְׂרָאֵל אֶל יהוה, כִּי עִם יהוה הַחֶסֶד, וְהַרְבֵּה עִמּוֹ פְדוּת: וְהוּא יִפְדֶּה אֶת יִשְׂרָאֵל מִכֹּל עֲוֹנֹתָיו:

[Say seven times:]

לְעוֹלָם יהוה דְּבָרְךָ נִצָּב בַּשָּׁמָיִם:

יְהִי רָצוֹן מִלְּפָנֶיךָ שֶׁעַל יְדֵי הֶאָרַת תִּקּוּנִים עַתִּיקָא קַדִּישָׁא דְּעַתִּיקִין בְּזְעֵיר שֶׁבְּבָארֶיךָ יְכֻבְּשׁוּ רַחֲמֶיךָ אֶת כַּעַסְךָ וְיָגֹלּוּ רַחֲמֶיךָ עַל מִדּוֹתֶיךָ וְתִתְנַהֵג עִמָּנוּ בְּמִדַּת הָרַחֲמִים. וְתִתֶּן לָנוּ חַיִּים אֲרוּכִים וְטוֹבִים בְּעִסְקֵי תוֹרָתֶךָ וְקִיּוּם מִצְוֹתֶיךָ לַעֲשׂוֹת רְצוֹנֶךָ אָמֵן כֵּן יְהִי רָצוֹן:

The designation יָה, *Yah*, is only half of HASHEM's full Name, יהוה, *the Dispenser of Mercy*. When Israel lives an incomplete, tortured existence in exile, HASHEM's Name is also incomplete (*Eruvin* 18b).

The Psalmist exclaims: HASHEM, when Israel is in exile, Your Attribute of Mercy is incomplete; only when the Temple stands and Israel is in its land is Your Goodness revealed in its full magnificence. But if You keep precise account of our sins, our merits will never be sufficient for us to emerge from exile unscathed (*Sforno*).

If You keep constant *account* of our sins and demand instant punishment, we will not have the opportunity to repent. If so, *who can withstand* the precise and exacting demands of Your Justice? (*Nevei Shalom*).

אֲדֹנָי מִי יַעֲמֹד — *My Lord, who could withstand?*

In exile we are bowed and bent in shame; we have fallen to the depths. The prophet (*Amos* 5:2) laments: *The maiden of Israel is fallen; she shall rise no more; she is abandoned on her soil, there is no one to raise her.*

O Lord, who can withstand Your anger at such a time? (*Alshich*).

כִּי עִמְּךָ הַסְּלִיחָה — *For with You is the forgiveness.*

Although You exercised Your control over This World through angels and spiritual intermediaries, You have retained the power of forgiveness for Yourself (*Rashi*), lest people say, 'We can sin with impunity, because the angels can be persuaded to forgive us.'

Therefore, in order *that You* [alone] *may be feared*, people must realize that You and none other can forgive them (*Radak*).

לְמַעַן תִּוָּרֵא — *So that You may be feared.*

If God did not forgive sins, then all men would be discouraged and broken. In fact, this despondent attitude would not hinder sin, but encourage it, because sinners would reason, 'We might as well commit crimes without restraint, because we are doomed anyway.'

However, since men can *find forgiveness in You*, they entertain hopes for a bright future even after they err. Consequently, they are afraid to sin against You [again], lest they ruin their chances for repentance (*Sefer Halk-karim* 4:26; *Akeidah* 92; *Maharshal*, cited in *Tzeidah LaDerech*).

קִוִּיתִי ה' קִוְּתָה נַפְשִׁי — *I placed confidence in HASHEM, my soul placed confidence.*

Time and again, I trusted only in HASHEM. The Psalmist says elsewhere (*Psalms* 27:14): קַוֵּה אֶל ה' חֲזַק וְיַאֲמֵץ לִבֶּךָ, *Place confidence in HASHEM* וְקַוֵּה אֶל ה',

with You is the forgiveness, so that You may be feared. I placed confidence in HASHEM, my soul placed confidence, and for His word I hoped. My soul is my Lord's, it is among the watchers for the morning, who watch for the morning. Let Israel hope for HASHEM, for with HASHEM is the kindness, and with Him there is great power of redemption. And it is He Who will redeem Israel from all its iniquities.

[Say seven times]:

Forever, HASHEM, Your word stands firm in heaven [Psalms 119:89].

May it be Your will that by means of the illuminating perfections of the ancient Holy One which are eternal in the microcosm of infinitude that Your mercy may conquer Your anger and Your mercy may overwhelm Your attributes. May You comport Yourself toward us with Your Attribute of Mercy, and may You grant us a long and good life engaged in the study of Your Torah, and performance of Your commandments, to do Your will. Amen. May such be Your will.

strengthen yourself and He will give you courage; and place confidence in HASHEM (Rashi).

I placed confidence in HASHEM to provide for my temporary physical needs, and my soul placed confidence in HASHEM to provide for its eternal spiritual needs (Ibn Yachya).

וְלִדְבָרוֹ הוֹחָלְתִּי — And for His word I hoped.

Malbim differentiates between תִּקְוָה, which refers to confidence even in the absence of an articulated promise, and יִחוּל, which refers to the hope that an expressed pledge will be fulfilled. The soul, because of its spiritual essence, naturally and instinctively places confidence in HASHEM even though He gives no explicit guarantee. The psalmist observes that this instinctive confidence would be sufficient cause for trust in the Almighty. However, there is another compelling reason for trust: God has given us דְּבָרוֹ, His word.

נַפְשִׁי לַאדֹנָי מִשֹּׁמְרִים לַבֹּקֶר — My soul is my Lord's, it is among the watchers for the morning.

[Our translation renders the prefix מ of מִשֹּׁמְרִים as מִן, among.]

Devout men arise early and await the morning so that they can begin their daily prayers to God at the earliest possible time (Radak). Similarly, the Jews languishing in exile eagerly watch for the dawn of redemption when they can better serve Him (Rashi).

Others explain the prefix מ as יוֹתֵר מִן, 'more than those' who watch for the morning. The night watchmen anxiously await the dawn because then they can rest from their arduous nightly vigil; our desire for God's closeness is even greater than that (Metzudas David).

[Israel, however, longs for the dawn of redemption because then Jews can reawaken their spiritual potential, that lay dormant during the long, black night of exile.]

He who awaits the arrival of another man is not completely confident, because he is apprehensive lest the man change his mind. He who awaits the dawn, however, has no doubts whatsoever that nature will follow its course and that the sun will rise. Nevertheless, says the psalmist, Israel's confidence in the advent of God's redemption even surpasses mankind's confidence in the daily recurrence of daybreak (R' Yosef Albo; Malbim).

שֹׁמְרִים לַבֹּקֶר — Who watch for the morning.

The repetition of this phrase signifies that Israel repeatedly awaits the dawn of redemption [without ever losing hope] (Rashi).

יַחֵל יִשְׂרָאֵל אֶל ה' — Let Israel hope for HASHEM.

Let Israel hope that He alone should redeem them (Rashi).

כִּי עִם ה' הַחֶסֶד — For with HASHEM is the kindness.

Since God is constantly dealing kindly with all of His creations, why should He act differently towards Israel? (Radak).

God even bestows His kindness upon those who are undeserving, because His love is great. Therefore, Israel can hope for God's kindness under all circumstances (Sforno).

Moreover, there is no point in turning to any other source for kindness for [only] with HASHEM is their [genuine] kindness. Prayer addressed to any other source is futile (R' Yosef Albo).

וְהַרְבֵּה עִמּוֹ פְדוּת — And with Him there is great power of redemption.

We can rely on God because He has already redeemed us time and again: from Egypt, from Babylonia, and from countless misfortunes (Radak).

Therefore, no matter how bleak and hopeless our situation appears, let Israel never give up hope, because God has already redeemed us from many other desperate situations (Sforno).

Midrash Eliyahu observes that when Jews are in exile, God accompanies them and shares in their suffering. We may rest assured that the redemption will come, for it is a kindness not only for us, but also — with HASHEM there is kindness — for God Himself, so˙to speak. Indeed, with Him there is great [relief at the time of] redemption.

וְהוּא יִפְדֶּה אֶת יִשְׂרָאֵל מִכֹּל עֲוֹנֹתָיו — And it is He who will redeem Israel from all its iniquities.

One might ask, 'How can God redeem Israel if it is still soiled by sin and filled with iniquity?' The answer is that God will first arouse the sincere desire to repent. Then He will forgive all of Israel's sins and redeem it from all its iniquities. Only then will He gather all the scattered exiles of Israel (Radak).

◆§ לְעוֹלָם ה' דְּבָרְךָ נִצָּב בַּשָּׁמָיִם — Forever, HASHEM, Your word stands firm in heaven.

At the time of Creation You said but a word, and a firmament appeared in the heavens! This accomplishment endures לְעוֹלָם, forever, for the stars and the celestial legions stand firm for all time (Radak).

Alshich observes that when a mortal utters a word, it immediately vanishes into thin air. The word of God, however, emanates in a holy fire which is not consumed or dissipated. Elsewhere (Psalms 33:6) the psalmist declares: By the word of HASHEM the heavens were made, and by the breath of His mouth all their host. God's breath is part of Him. Just as He is eternal, so is His breath and His word.

Similarly, Isaiah (40:8) says: The grass withers, the flower fades, but the word of our God shall stand forever (Midrash Shocher Tov).

Moreover, Pesikta Rabbasi (40) derives from the use in our verse of the Four-Letter Name, that it is as the Dispenser of Mercy that HASHEM stands firm forever, even when He sits in judgment and exercises His Attribute of Strict Justice.

This has been the case since the very dawn of Creation. The universe was created on the twenty-fifth day of Elul. Six days later, on the first of Tishrei, Adam was brought forth from the earth. On that very day he sinned. Although God was filled with wrath, He did not destroy Adam, because He tempered His anger with the attribute of HASHEM, Dispenser of Mercy.

HASHEM stands firm in His practice of exercising mercy לְעוֹלָם, forever. Thus he displays it every year, on the first of Tishrei, which He ordained as Rosh Hashanah, the day when all creatures pass in judgment before Him.